STYLE TRENDS
OF PUEBLO POTTERY
1500 - 1840

BY

H. P. MERA

With an introduction by
Jonathan Batkin

Avanyu Publishing Inc.

Original material ©1939 by Laboratory of Anthropology,
The Museum of New Mexico, Santa Fe, N.M.
New Material ©1991 by Avanyu Publishing Inc.

AVANYU PUBLISHING INC.
P.O. Box 27134
Albuquerque, NM 87125
(505)243-8485
(505)266-6128

Library of Congress Cataloging-in-Publication Data

Mera, H.P. (Harry Percival), 1875-1951.
      Style trends of Pueblo pottery, 1500-1840 / by H.P. Mera ; with an introduc-
tion by Jonathan Batkin.
            p.   cm.
      Reprint. Originally published: Style trends of Pueblo pottery in the Rio
Grande and Little Colorado cultural areas from the sixteenth to the nineteenth century.
1939. Originally published in series: Memoirs of the Laboratory of Anthropology ; v. 3
      Includes bibliographical references.
      ISBN 0-936755-18-0
      1. Pueblo Indians--Pottery. 2. Pueblo Indians--Antiquities. 3. Pottery--New
Mexico--Classification. 4. Pottery--New Mexico--Themes, motives. 5. New Mexico--
Antiquities. I. Title.   E99.P9M413 1991
978.9'01--dc20
                                                                        91-10311
                                                                        CIP

PREFACE

Avanyu Publishing continues its quest to bring into print manuscripts which will contribute to the education of collectors, dealers, and students alike.

We are extremely pleased to present our first title on Pueblo pottery. While considering several previously published manuscripts as potential reprint possibilities, we inquired of Bruce Bernstein, then associated with the Wheelwright Museum in Santa Fe, and Jonathan Batkin, then associated with the Southwest Museum in Los Angeles, their recommendations on which of these books was the most worthwhile to bring back in print. Both were so enthusiastic about Mera's *Style Trends of Pueblo Pottery* that we chose it.

Batkin readily agreed to our request that he write an introduction to the new edition and Bernstein was equally enthusiastic about assisting us in gaining proper approval from the Laboratory of Anthropology, which held the copyright to the 1939 edition, and in preparing a foreword to this edition. We appreciate the generous assistance by both and we are pleased to acknowledge their efforts.

We have reproduced the original book in its entirety, including the original dust jacket. The only changes made to the original manuscript were to correct the errors presumed to have been made in 1939 in which Mera's black outline drawings for plates VIII and LXVI were apparently switched. We have put them where Mera obviously meant them to be.

We hope the many collectors and students of historic period pottery from the pueblos of New Mexico enjoy this book and that it provides an inspiration to them to further their interest in this area.

Alexander E. Anthony, Jr.   J. Brent Ricks

FOREWORD

It is a great pleasure to present the long overdue re-publication of one of the singularly most influential works concerning Pueblo pottery. Mera's work continues to serve as the foundation for understanding the nomenclature and developmental sequence of historic Pueblo pottery. The book remains the definitive statement on historic pottery. There are some minor revisions (see Batkin's introduction in this edition), but these build on Mera's work rather than reformulate it. Finally, every appreciator of pottery has benefitted from this ground-breaking work whether by reading Mera's own fine, crisp prose or by reading any subsequent work written about historic Pueblo pottery. As appreciators of pottery, we all owe a debt of gratitude to Harry Mera. As inheritors of his work, we may tend to forget how recently it was that little was known about Pueblo pottery.

It took diligence and vision to write *Style Trends of Pueblo Pottery*. Mera wrote of this quest, "[pottery] appeared incapable of being arranged in any semblance of order, either as to time or genetic relationship" (p. vi). Mera's method of thinking through problems is evident in his collection of data. He would often go to the historic record to find abandoned pueblos that represented the precise time frame necessary to locate a piece of the developmental puzzle he sought to put together. Further, with Kenneth Chapman he scoured the Pueblos searching for pots and other information. His depth of knowledge and writing tell us he was constantly questioning living Pueblo people too. It took Mera at least ten years to accumulate the data necessary to write *Style Trends*.

His accomplishment is all the more remarkable in the context of his life. He was trained in medicine and began his second career in archaeology, without benefit of formal training. Perhaps as a result of his background, he was a humanist, consistently calling attention to the role of the individual in the development and maintenance of artistic traditions.

Mera first came to New Mexico with his brother, Frank Mera, helping to found Sunmount Sanatorium for tubercular patients. After a brief stay he set up practice in Abilene, Kansas, but continued paying frequent visits to Santa Fe. He settled permanently in Santa Fe in 1922, serving as county health officer. By 1923 he was among the group that founded the Pueblo Pottery Fund (later known as the Indian Arts Fund) to save choice older examples of pottery for permanent exhibition in Santa Fe. He also began his archaeological survey and sherd collections, which today, at the Museum of

FOREWORD

Indian Arts and Culture/Laboratory of Anthropology, continue to be regarded as keystones of southwestern anthropological research.[1] In 1929 he left medicine to become the first curator of archaeology at the newly established Laboratory of Anthropology.

These were to be prolific years. In the course of a few years, he was able to put together developmental and temporal sequences for Southwestern pottery, jewelry, and textiles that continue to be seminal to our understanding of Southwestern Indian arts and culture. Mera, or "Doc" as he was known, also did the photography and art work for his publications. Between 1929 and his death in 1951 he published three books and 32 major papers.

In a draft of a late 1930s letter in the Laboratory of Anthropology archives[2] requesting funding for publication of the Memoirs series in which *Style Trends of Pueblo Pottery* was volume III, Mera summarized the importance of his work:

> Ever since attention was first drawn to the Southwest, through the Hemenway Expedition and the Bureau of American Ethnology and others in the 1870s and 1880s, scores of volumes have appeared on the archaeology of the region. In all of these, ceramics are the outstanding feature, yet during the same period the ceramics of the living pueblos have passed almost unnoticed.
>
> Only one well illustrated report on the general subject of the Pueblo pottery had appeared until 1924, when Guthe's[3] work on the technology of pottery making at San Ildefonso directed attention to the little known field. The neglect of this important phase in Pueblo art is apparently due to the mistaken conclusion that their pottery of the post-Spanish period (1540 to date) was influenced largely by Spanish contacts, and that it had not the value inherent in the wares of prehistoric times. The fallacy of such conclusions has now been shown, for there is almost no trace of the copying of extraneous ideas in the pottery decoration of the past centuries. Though some pueblos are within easy visiting distance from each other, each has long since developed its own style so that its pottery can be identified readily by material, form, color, and decoration. To add to the variety, the pottery of certain pueblos cannot be arranged in a sequence covering several centuries so that scope of each proves much wider than previously believed.
>
> To the Laboratory of Anthropology goes the credit for publishing in 1936, in its Memoirs series, the first volume ever to feature fully the

---

[1]The archaeological survey continues to grow and currently contains a record of over 75,000 New Mexico archaeological sites. The sherd collections continue to serve as the type collections of the Southwestern ceramic sequence.

[2]Laboratory of Anthropology archives (#89LA 4.035.2).

[3]Carl E. Guthe (1925), *Pueblo Pottery Making: A Study at the Village of San Ildefonso*.

decorative art in the ceramics of a living pueblo.[4] It was planned to follow this promptly with a series on the ceramics of the other pottery-making pueblos but until recently the acquiring of desirable specimens held in Pueblo homes, and the need for a complete photographic survey of the pottery already in the principal museums of America, have tended to retard the project....

The work will also provide for the first time one authentic identification of the wares of each pueblo, a much needed service that will displace the misinformation recorded in early days by collectors who casually attributed each find to the pueblo from which it was acquired, unmindful of the promiscuous trading which continues to this day.

Pottery appreciators, scholars, and newcomers are all indebted to Harry Mera and his meticulously crafted *Style Trends of Pueblo Pottery* work and, further, we are grateful that Avanyu Publishing Inc. is providing such fine service to the field through the re-publication of his work.

Bruce Bernstein
Assistant Director and Chief Curator
Laboratory of Anthropology/Museum of Indian Arts and Culture

[4]There were only four published volumes in the Memoirs of the Laboratory of Anthropology Series. Volume I, which Mera is referring to here is Kenneth Chapman's *The Pottery of Santo Domingo Pueblo* (1938). The volumes were Mera's *"Rain Bird:" A Study in Pueblo Design, Volume II* (1938), and Mera's *Pueblo Indian Embroidery, Volume IV* (1943). Each of these works, along with *Style Trends of Pueblo Pottery, Volume III* (1939) is a classic and irreplaceable study.

INTRODUCTION

by Jonathan Batkin

This classic, pioneering work focuses on New Mexico Pueblo pottery made, in the author's words, "from some time in the 16th Century on into the early part of the 19th." If we were to assign specific dates, we might choose 1500 to 1840, because the earliest vessels illustrated here are examples of types made shortly before the Spanish first explored the region, and the latest are examples of types known from excavation of Pecos, which was abandoned in 1838. In the fifty-two years since it was published, this book has become scarce and has unfortunately come to be overlooked by many students of Pueblo pottery. Perhaps this reprint will bring long overdue credit to Harry Mera for his innovations that we take for granted today.

Mera acknowledged the limitations of this study by use of the word "trends." A definitive analysis of pottery styles from 1500 to 1840 is nearly impossible, because whole vessels from the period are rare. It has been proposed by some authors (not Mera) that this rarity is the result of a Spanish ban on the burial of pottery with the dead. No evidence of any such prohibition exists and, in actuality, the Pueblos had ceased placing large quantities of pottery in burials before the Spanish arrived. Natural attrition is really the reason for this rarity. Most vessels are used until broken and deposited in the village trash heap. Almost all the pueblos occupied since the Spanish Reconquest of the 1690s are still occupied, and excavations in them have been extremely limited; thus, even fragmentary vessels made between 1700 and 1870, when museums began to collect, are scarce. Only a few complete early historic vessels survived as heirlooms or were preserved in abandoned storerooms.

Consequently this book is limited in two ways: only trends are described, and only types represented by whole or nearly whole examples are illustrated. This is not to say that Mera did not study sherds. To the contrary, the great value of his research lies in the fact that he depended on sherds and sought them from sites occupied during known, brief periods. Four sites occupied at the end of the 17th Century provided Mera valuable information. These were the Jemez village of Astialakwa, destroyed by the Spanish in 1694; Black Mesa, where the people of San Ildefonso sustained a seven-month siege the same year; Kotyiti, occupied by the people of Cochiti from 1680 to 1694; and a village near San Felipe, temporarily occupied during the same period as Kotyiti. Also important for Mera was a large group of reconstructed 18th-Century vessels from Pueblo refuge sites in

1

Gobernador Canyon of northwestern New Mexico, now at the University of Colorado Museum.

By examining vessels and sherds, Mera was able to establish a chronology for the trends he perceived. When Mera wrote this book, the only scholarly analysis of Pueblo pottery that had been published was *The Pottery of Pecos* by Alfred Vincent Kidder and others.[1] Though Kidder and his collaborators relied on a wide variety of features in their analyses, they chose the shape of bowl rims as the principal index of chronology. Mera was not only familiar with this method, he had published results of some of his own research on prehistoric glaze pottery in 1933, using bowl rim shape to illustrate his observations.[2]

Nevertheless, this method of analysis was inadequate for demonstrating the changes in pottery since Spanish contact. Instead, Mera chose the *olla*, or water jar, as his index of chronology. Mera herein explains the abandonment, throughout the Pueblo world over a period of about 150 years, of flattened jar shapes with rounded bases, and the adoption of taller forms with indented bases. He locates the origin of this trend in the upper Rio Grande region. He also describes the spread from west to east of stylized feather motifs as popular decorative elements.

Concepts about early historic pottery presented in this book may appear so elementary to readers familiar with recent literature that they may not realize the ideas were first proposed here by Mera. He identified and named several early historic pottery types, established the chronology that we follow today, and plotted the boundaries of ceramic provinces in the historic period.

In the years since this was published, formerly unknown historic sites have been excavated and many more people have taken an interest in early historic pottery. Consequently, some elements of Mera's typology have been changed, but not always rightly so. Errors by Mera have also surfaced and of those, he acknowledged the ones that came to light before his death. I take this opportunity to discuss some of them, not to take issue with Mera, but to help serious new students overlook them.

Three pieces illustrated in plates XXVII through XXIX are misidentified and/or misdated. Those in plates XXVII and XXVIII are both much later than the period under study. The former has a shape and decoration attributable to Santo Domingo between 1880 and 1920; the latter has a shape popular at San Ildefonso between about 1900 and 1920. Both have rag-polished bentonite slip, which supports the later dates. Though Mera considered their shapes the same as that of the Kotyiti Glaze Polychrome jar in plate XXXIV, they are significantly different. The jar in plate XXIX was certainly made in the 18th Century, but at Zuni rather than in the upper Rio Grande region.

[1]Kidder, Alfred Vincent, "The Pottery of Pecos. Volume I: The Dull-Paint Wares, with a Section on the Black-on-white Wares by Charles Avery Amsden," *Papers of the Southwestern Expedition* 5, 1931; Kidder, Alfred Vincent, and Anna O. Shepard, "The Pottery of Pecos. Volume II. 1: The Glaze-Paint, Culinary and Other Wares. 2: The Technology of Pecos Pottery," *Papers of the Southwestern Expedition* 7, 1936 (New Haven: Published for Phillips Academy by Yale University Press).

[2]Mera, H. P. "A Proposed Revision of the Rio Grande Glaze Paint Sequence," *Laboratory of Anthropology Technical Series, Bulletin* 5 (Santa Fe, 1933).

Some other vessels would today be identified by other type names, but this does not mean that Mera was wrong. He was merely cautious. For example, he recognized the relatedness of the Acoma, Laguna, and Zuni ceramic traditions and chose to "lump" their 18th- and early 19th-Century vessels under the name Ashiwi Polychrome. For many years, scholars questioned the utility of the name, and it was eventually redefined by Francis Harlow, who has contributed substantially to our knowledge of early historic pottery. Harlow demonstrated that pottery of Acoma or Laguna is readily separable from that of Zuni. He preserved Mera's name, Ashiwi Polychrome, for Zuni vessels, and created Ako Polychrome and other names for vessels from Acoma and Laguna. We should not disregard Mera's caution, however. He elsewhere described some problematic vessels or sherds as "acni ['Acoma-Zuni']," and I admit to being stumped by similar things.

One of Mera's statements that may be incorrect has yet to be proven wrong. He describes Posuge Red specifically as a Tewa jar type, but I have seen no evidence to prove its existence. Polished red bowls, soup plates, and other forms are common in sites dating from the late 17th Century to the early 19th Century, but not a single fragment of an indisputable Posuge Red jar is known. Numerous red neck fragments can be found, but I have seen these in association with either painted, white-slipped midbody fragments or no midbody fragments at all. In other words, it appears that red neck fragments are invariably from jars of the type Mera named Pojoaque Polychrome.

Mera's most confusing error was in his selection of an example to illustrate the type he called Tewa Polychrome. This error led to misunderstanding by other scholars and to unnecessary complication of the Tewa ceramic sequence. Although he made the error in this volume, he had clearly defined Tewa Polychrome seven years earlier.[3]

What Mera proposed was quite simple: a long continuum of white-slipped Tewa pottery began in prehistoric times on the Pajarito Plateau with the type called Biscuit Ware. By around 1550, Mera determined, Biscuit Ware had given way at Pajarito Plateau sites such as Sankawi and Tsirege to a new type, Sankawi Black-on-cream. This type was similar in outer appearance to Biscuit Ware, but the clay and temper were quite different: the new ware was thinner and harder, and the paste was light brown. The paste is, in fact, identical to that still employed by potters of Tewa villages. By the late 17th Century, Sankawi Black-on-cream began to evolve further. The rims of jars were now slipped red, and their bases treated with either a red band or perhaps a solid covering of red slip. This type, slightly evolved from Sankawi Black-on-cream, is what Mera named Tewa Polychrome. It is a rare type known almost exclusively from fragments of water jars from late 17th-Century sites.

When Mera published *Style Trends* he mistakenly illustrated a fragment of a Pojoaque Polychrome jar as an example of his Tewa Polychrome type (plate XV); careful scrutiny of the fragment later revealed that the tall upperbody of the jar was red and not white. Mera admitted the error and approved a slightly revised

[3]Mera, H. P., "Wares Ancestral to Tewa Polychrome," *Laboratory of Anthropology Technical Series Bulletin* 4 (Santa Fe, 1932).

definition of Tewa Polychrome by archaeologist Joseph Toulouse in 1949.[4] Mera's error has been compounded by misunderstanding over the years, but further discussion is beyond the scope of this introduction. The interested reader can turn elsewhere for details.[5]

When Harry Mera began studying early historic pottery more than sixty years ago, he was almost alone in his enthusiasm for these beautiful objects, and I am sure he would be delighted to know that hundreds of people admire them today. I can only hope that some of the new enthusiasts will now acknowledge his important contributions.

[4]Toulouse, Joseph H., Jr., "The Mission of San Gregorio de Abo: A Report on the Excavation and Repair of a Seventeenth-Century New Mexico Mission," *Monographs of the School of American Research* 13 (Santa Fe, 1949), p.20.

[5]Batkin, Jonathan, *Pottery of the Pueblos of New Mexico, 1700-1940* (Colorado Springs: The Taylor Museum of the Colorado Springs Fine Arts Center, 1987), pp. 37-39.

BY H. P. MERA

STYLE TRENDS OF

PUEBLO POTTERY

LABORATORY OF ANTHROPOLOGY
SANTA FÉ NEW MEXICO

STYLE TRENDS
OF PUEBLO POTTERY

IN THE

Rio Grande and Little Colorado
Cultural Areas from the Sixteenth
to the Nineteenth Century

BY

H. P. MERA

Memoirs of the
Laboratory of Anthropology
Volume III

Santa Fé, New Mexico

1939

A contribution from the American Council of Learned Societies has assisted in the publication of this volume

Composed and Printed at the
WAVERLY PRESS, INC.
Baltimore, Md., U. S. A.

CONTENTS

iii

PLATES

FOREWORD

Although the writer, through a rather intimate acquaintance with an extensive collection of Pueblo pottery, had for some years past been made to realize that there were a number of very distinctive styles incident to the historic period, these, at the time, appeared incapable of being arranged in any semblance of order, either as to time or genetic relationship.

But following a study of sherd material, secured while conducting an archaeological survey which covered a large number of sites representative of all ages, some light began to be thrown on the question. By following the clues thus obtained, a much more lucid situation was developed from which a number of conclusions were drawn. These will be found embodied in the paper herewith presented.

In the matter of locating entire vessels to match certain classes of sherds, apparently representative of style periods, access to collections and information concerning needed specimens has been freely and generously afforded by several institutions and individuals. Illustrative material, other than that taken from the collections of the Indian Arts Fund and the Laboratory of Anthropology, with which organizations the author is associated, has been furnished by Dr. N. C. Nelson and the American Museum of Natural History, Mr. Donald Scott and the Peabody Museum at Harvard University, Mr. E. H. Morris and the Museum of the University of Colorado, Mr. Neil M. Judd and the United States National Museum, Mr. F. H. Douglas and Miss Betsy Forbes of the Denver Art Museum, Mr. Herman Schweizer and the Fred Harvey Co., Dr. F. E. Mera, Mr. Sheldon Parsons and Miss Olive Rush. To these and to all others who have been of assistance, grateful acknowledgment is here made.

However, all the effort spent in this undertaking would have been largely without effect were it not for the funds generously provided by The American Council of Learned Societies toward publication.

H. P. M.

PART I

DEVELOPMENT OF FORM

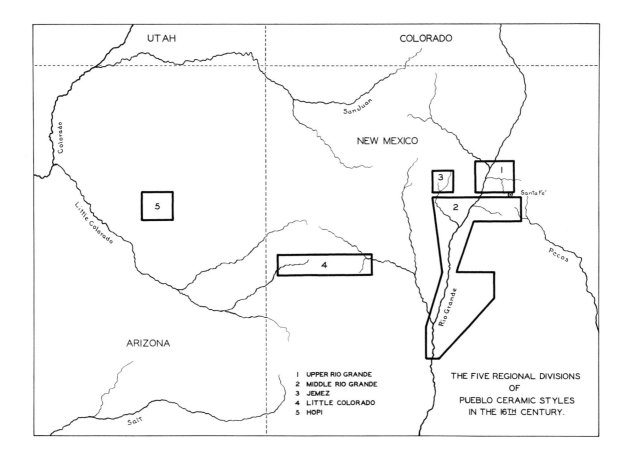

UTAH   COLORADO

NEW MEXICO

Colorado

San Juan

Little Colorado

Santa Fe'

Pecos

Rio Grande

ARIZONA

Salt

1 UPPER RIO GRANDE
2 MIDDLE RIO GRANDE
3 JEMEZ
4 LITTLE COLORADO
5 HOPI

THE FIVE REGIONAL DIVISIONS
OF
PUEBLO CERAMIC STYLES
IN THE 16TH CENTURY.

INTRODUCTION

A number of very interesting and intimately connected ceramic developments, occurring during the Spanish domination of the Pueblo area, have heretofore received little attention. These several series of evolutionary progressions, that constitute the subject of this study, took place over a span of years extending from sometime in the 16th Century on into the early part of the 19th.

The neglect of so important a chapter in the history of Southwestern aboriginal pottery-making is believed to have been due largely to the paucity of dateable material, other than sherds, upon which would depend a successful tracing of the line of descent and sequences for the various developmental stages. Whole vessels, or any capable of restoration, surviving from this period are comparatively few in number. The principal reason for such a scarcity lies in the fact that a large proportion of those villages coming within the time range where desired material might be expected to be recovered, have been continuously occupied since at least the beginning of the 18th Century. Hence, due to a readily understandable prejudice on the part of the inhabitants, no opportunity has been offered for excavation.

Fortunately, however, there are a few definitely dated sites that were abandoned during or soon after the Pueblo Rebellion of 1680 A.D. and others which were only temporarily occupied at that time or in the following century, from which both sherds and a small number of complete vessels are available. For the purposes of the present study such sites offer the most satisfactory evidence because there exists no danger of confusion with either earlier or later periods. Despite such a comparative dearth of available evidence, it has been found possible, by means of sherds and the few surviving whole specimens, to present at least an outline of the trends in pottery styles during a period in which occurred what was undoubtedly one of the most wide-spread disturbances that Pueblo social organization has been destined to withstand. As a consequence, the unstabilized condition of that period is to be found plainly reflected in the nature of both shapes and designs which link the fashions of the late prehistoric with those of more modern times.

Before dealing with the main theme, it will be advisable to supply a background compiled from various archaeological sources, so that lines of descent may be the more intelligently traced.

The territory occupied by pueblo-dwelling peoples in the early part of the 16th Century can be divided into five geographical areas on the basis of certain easily distinct and distinguishable ceramic specializations. (See map.) These are presented in order from east to west, with brief explanations.

THE FIVE CERAMIC PROVINCES IN LATE PREHISTORIC TIMES

UPPER RIO GRANDE CERAMIC PROVINCE

The principal and most characteristic pottery type native to this district in late prehistoric times has been termed Biscuit ware.[1] A matte black paint derived from a vegetal source was employed for the purposes of decoration. This was applied on a light colored slip usually having a grayish cast or more rarely verging toward a tan. Patterns were based on geometric forms descended from earlier Black-on-white styles. Depressed, somewhat flattened olla shapes were the rule. The bottoms of both jars and bowls were rounded (plates I, II and III).

MIDDLE RIO GRANDE CERAMIC PROVINCE

Some time in the 14th Century, the manufacture of a red ware decorated with a crude lead-glaze paint began in this district. This had been adapted from a type then the prevailing fashion in the Little Colorado area to the west. By the addition of white, yellowish and tan slips a polychrome was achieved which eventually became the accepted usage.[2] Here also depressed jar forms with rounding bottoms were standard. Bottoms of bowls conformed to those of jars (plates IV, V and VI).

Incidentally, the ceramic culture of the pueblos of Taos and Picuris, the two northernmost villages in New Mexico, was originally one with that of the Middle Rio Grande province, but on examination of sherd material from their middens it appears that, possibly as late as the early part of the 16th Century, traditional styles were discarded in favor of an Apache-like pottery which has been the only type since produced. Hence these two pueblos may be considered as apart from the present problem.

JEMEZ CERAMIC PROVINCE

A rather simple Black-on-white type survived in this small district, little altered from primitive ancestral forms. Because it was not greatly affected by and as it exerted no appreciable influence on neighboring developments, which are the principal interest of this study, this type may be eliminated from further discussion. Jemez pottery became extinct in the early years of the 18th Century. Two examples are shown on plates VII and VIII.

LITTLE COLORADO CERAMIC PROVINCE

Here also a basic red-ware complex dominated the region in the latter centuries of prehistoric times; one that was directly responsible, as before stated, for the red-ware popularity in the Middle Rio Grande. Although a red slip appears to have been particularly esteemed, white or cream colored varieties were not uncommon.

[1] Kidder and Amsden, Part II, 1931; Mera, 1934.
[2] Kidder and Shepard, 1936.

Decorative patterns were achieved by means of an impure lead-glaze paint with colors ranging from greens of varying shades, through the browns to a dense black. Although certain features such as rim forms and other details differed considerably from those of all other districts, jar shapes in general agreed by having diameters usually greater than the height. Also, rounded bottoms for these as well as bowls were characteristic (plates IX and X).

HOPI CERAMIC PROVINCE

Widely differing in appearance from all other wares produced in Pueblo territory is the yellow or orange colored pottery that had its origin in this westernmost district, and which, from the time of its inception, has appeared in an uninterrupted succession of types down to the present day. Unfortunately, few studies have been made of any developmental steps occurring in this ware since the arrival of the Spanish in the 16th Century and although closely connected with the present subject, especially as a source of certain eastward spreading features of design, it must be largely omitted from this paper. Before entirely dismissing the matter however, it is of interest to note that here too jars followed the favored fashion of the times for flattened shapes with rounding bottoms.

After reviewing the above brief synopsis, it becomes at once evident that despite widely differing ideas concerning the choice of paint, color and character of slip in the several provinces, two basic features were common to all except the Jemez area where water jars offer an exception but, as previously explained, the pottery of that region does not enter into the present question. The two are depressed olla forms and round bottomed vessels. Emphasis has been placed on this uniformity in order to draw attention to a number of revolutionary changes in ceramic styles which later took place.

But before beginning a discussion of these changes it perhaps will be well to again digress and call attention to something of the attendant conditions affecting the social and economic situation during which such marked alterations in style took place.

CONDITIONS OF SOCIETY AFFECTING CERAMICS DURING THE SPANISH COLONIAL PERIOD

Though authentic figures concerning the number of occupied villages existing at the time of Coronado's arrival in 1540 are lacking, an approximation may be obtained by averaging the several conflicting counts made by various chroniclers at different times during the years of conquest. By this method, a figure lying somewhere between seventy and eighty appears to constitute a conservative estimate.

It is generally accepted that, even prior to the appearance of the Spanish in 1540, a decrease in population over the Pueblo region had been steadily taking place, due, it is believed, to attacks by incoming nomadic peoples, to disease resulting from lack of proper sanitation, and to internecine strife. But after settlement had been effected by European conquerors, this decline became so greatly accelerated that by the middle of the 18th Century only some twenty-three towns are known to have survived in the entire Pueblo area, with a number of very small, temporary settlements founded by refugees scattered far to the north in Navajo territory. Two principal factors seem to have been involved in the steady shrinkage of population which took place while colonization was in progress. One was the loss of life incident to the many and constantly recurring minor uprisings which were ruthlessly put down; the other, probably nearly as great a cause of mortality, and one which may have also acted as a deterrent to repopulation as well, can be seen in various forms of peonage and exploitation to which the Indians of that period were subjected.

The notorious *encomienda*[3] system, designed to force Christianity on the aborigines, was in force during this time. Under the terms of this plan Indians of both sexes could be legally drafted from their villages in considerable numbers by officials and settlers of standing, to repay in labor the spiritual guidance and necessities of life presumed to be supplied by the *patrón*. Abuse of this system led to virtual slavery. Besides domestic employment and labor in the fields, sweatshops are known to have been maintained in which great quantities of cotton and woolen fabrics were produced for trade with Mexico. Pottery making also continued throughout the years of bondage to be an important industry because, due to the difficulty of transportation from other sources, colonists were largely dependent on the supply of native wares for domestic use. Concentrations of this character made up of individuals and groups drawn from many communities, previously having had little or no contact with one another under normal conditions, may have furnished the means for an exchange of ideas which resulted in the spread of certain ceramic styles appearing during that period.

With this brief sketch concerning the social situation, attention will next be directed to the several progressive changes in style which took place during the years designated in the title of this study.

[3] Barbour, 1932.

DESCRIPTION

THE UPPER RIO GRANDE CERAMIC PROVINCE

What is believed to be the first departure from the normally depressed olla forms characteristic for all parts of the Pueblo area in the early 16th Century appears to have taken place among a small group of isolated, highland pueblos situated on the Pajarito Plateau, a section of country included in the Upper Rio Grande province. Therefore the principal objective of this paper can logically begin with a discussion of style evolution as it took place in this province.

SANKAWI BLACK-ON-CREAM

In one of these villages some genius defied convention and produced a pottery form that marked the beginning of new conceptions concerning vessel shapes, in that height to width ratios were greatly increased. From this beginning an influence eventually spread over the entire Pueblo region, giving rise to styles that were distinct from anything previously produced in the Southwest. The first result of this revolutionary move was the creation of a new pottery type, now known as Sankawi Black-on-cream,[4] which seems to have appeared fully developed without, curiously enough, any shapes that can be considered as transitional between it and its predecessor, Biscuit ware.

Another new feature, in addition to the gain in height ratio and a somewhat enlarged capacity obtained by means of a prolongation of the neck, is seen in the concave depression pushed up into the bottom, a complete reversal of the earlier fashion for the convexly rounded sort. Although such concave basal depressions are not unknown to Southwestern ceramics, at no time could this feature be said to have enjoyed extensive usage late enough to consider its appearance in the new type as a borrowed trait. Hence, as no immediate source has been discovered with which to connote so sudden an appearance, an independent invention may tentatively be postulated. Perhaps the increased height added so much to the difficulty of balancing this form of olla when carried on the head, that a hollow in the base might well aid in preserving equilibrium to a greater degree than that afforded by those braided yucca rings, indispensable in transporting round bottomed vessels in a like manner.

Olla rims of the Sankawi type have very little or no flare at all, though the lip itself has a slightly inward bevel.

With few exceptions, Sankawi bowls, though still retaining rounding base

---

[4] Mera, 1932.

contours, differ from Biscuit ware vessels of the same class by having direct unspecialized rims with a tendency to slightly incurve. But before continuing, it might be well to merely mention in passing that a form of specialized rim, one introduced from the Middle Rio Grande province to the south, is occasionally seen during the life of this type. However, because it appears only sporadically and becomes of major interest only during the next stage of development, further attention is reserved until it becomes more definitely identified with the Upper Rio Grande complex.

The two water jars and a bowl shown on plates XI, XII and XIII will give a clearer idea of form and a comparison of these with typical examples of Biscuit ware presented on plates I, II and III will at once demonstrate the several differences.

While making these comparisons, attention is also directed to the general similarity in design between the two types and although but little is known concerning the entire range covered by Sankawi decoration, the greatest difference between them may be said to lie in the quality of line work.

Broad lines and solidly filled spaces are much in evidence in Biscuit ware, while in the later type there is a general sense of lightness given to the whole decorative structure by the use of thin lines and proportionately smaller solid areas, though unfortunately the effectiveness of this treatment is quite often marred by poor draftsmanship.

In both, the principal design structure consists of a single band of decoration, bounded by one or more framing lines, encircling the vessel at its greatest circumference in the Sankawi type and just above that point in the case of Biscuit ware. This band may be interrupted completely, or at times only partially, by a vertical, so called "ceremonial break", a usual feature in the Sankawi type, but one more rarely seen in the earlier Biscuit. Though the name ceremonial break has been employed throughout this paper to describe an intentional gap in one or more of the framing lines of a design, it is admittedly a loose and inexact use of the term. Such interruptions appear to represent the observance of a custom relating to some form of belief, the nature of which does not seem to have been definitely established and in no way has reference to any particular ceremony or rite. However, that designation has been so thoroughly fixed through popular usage that it has here been retained.

In this same connection, another contingency arose as a result of the change to taller shapes, one which was to greatly influence the future character of pottery design. This was brought about by a considerable increase in the area which could be utilized for decorative purposes. However, at this particular stage little advantage was taken of such a possibility beyond the application of narrow decorative bands, or small detached figures, to the upper part of the neck just below the lip. At a slightly later period, it will be seen that full use was made of the increase in space.

No exact date for the earliest appearance of Sankawi Black-on-cream can be advanced. The only definite statement possible to make at this time is that about a decade after the middle of the 16th Century this type seems to have comprised the bulk of decorated pottery in use at three pueblos, Sankawi, Tsirege, and Puye, situated on the Pajarito Plateau. To substantiate this statement two dates are offered which were obtained, by means of dendrochronological studies, from timbers taken from the latter two villages. These indicate that either construction or the repair of rooms was still being undertaken as late as 1574, in the first instance, and 1568, in the other.[5] Hence, an allowance of a number of years prior to these dates must be made in estimating the first appearance of the Sankawi type.

After a lapse of time concerning which there is no record, the people of these towns for unknown reasons abandoned their highland homes and, according to credible Indian tradition, descended to the valley of the Rio Grande. Here they became incorporated with the several Tewa villages already located along the course of that stream, where they were first visited by the Spanish in 1540.

There can be no doubt but that the incoming uplanders brought with them their own pottery styles including the new tall olla forms, though perhaps these had already become more or less familiar to the valley dwellers through the medium of trade. However that may be, it is plainly seen that the introduced type finally gained a complete ascendency over the more squatty local shapes.

TEWA POLYCHROME

By the last quarter of the 17th Century the new style became, with some added features and modifications, the standard usage for the whole Upper Rio Grande province and in addition influenced or, in some instances, even threatened to replace the pottery fashions native to the neighboring Middle Rio Grande section.

In the case of water jars, the principal divergence from the ancestral Sankawi tradition was the addition of a polished red-slipped base which was carried up to a point just below the usual median band of decoration.

Another and even more surprising proceeding, taking place during this period, was the adoption of an entirely new bowl form borrowed from a Middle Rio Grande source. It will be remembered (page 10) that attention has been called previously to the sporadic appearance of an alien form at Sankawi Black-on-cream sites. These early examples were but the forerunners of a change by which bowls with the normally in-curving rims of the Sankawi type (plate XIII) were discarded in favor of those possessing this feature placed vertically, meeting the bowl curvature at an obtuse angle. Plate XIV illustrates an example of the new fashion and on plate XXXVI may be seen the Middle Rio Grande type from which it was inspired. As in ollas the entire under surface below the upright rim bears a polished red slip. Painted decoration on the usual cream colored ground is exclusively confined, as far as known, to the exterior surface of the rim. Interiors were polished but normally not slipped.

There was a great improvement over the preceding Sankawi type in the quality of draftsmanship and in increased delicacy of line. A matte carbon paint was em-

[5] Stallings, 1933, p. 805.

ployed, similar to that in use in this province from an early period and one that has continued in use without interruption, down to the present day.

Typical sherds of this early form of Tewa Polychrome are not uncommon and from these it has been possible to obtain a fairly comprehensive idea concerning its characteristics, but entire or even nearly complete vessels are extremely rare. A bowl and the basal portion of an olla shown on plates XIV and XV are the best examples known to the writer.

So far, all fragments of this type have been found in association with sites occupied during the latter part of the 17th Century. Probably one of the best of these for the purpose of examining authentic pottery fragments of that period, particularly because of the absence of sherd material from other occupations, is situated on the Black Mesa a short distance north of the pueblo of San Ildefonso. It was on the flat top of this volcanic butte that the Indians of that pueblo sustained a seven months' siege by the Spanish in the year 1694. The remains of houses and shelters built during that time may still be seen, around which, besides pieces of rough culinary ware, are to be found only sherds of Tewa Polychrome and those of a new type which now enters into the problem.

The first part of the term used to specify this type preserves the name of the linguistic group which predominates in the Upper Rio Grande province.

POSUGE RED

The new type appears to have come into existence sometime during this same general period as it has not yet been identified at less complex sites known to be much earlier than the latter part of the 17th Century.

Little definite information can be given concerning the full range of olla shapes incident to this new type because entire specimens have not yet been recovered. The curvature of some neck sherds indicates a long slope like that of Tewa Polychrome, others could only have belonged to jars having a form verging a little more toward the globular. A more detailed description of this type must await the result of some fortunate finds. There are, nevertheless, a few very evident features that mark it as a strictly different development. A highly polished red slip covered the whole exterior surface; this together with an outward flaring rim sets it quite apart from any other in the province existing on the same time level. For convenience the designation Posuge Red will hereinafter be used. Just where the type originated is problematical but it is noticeable that sherds of this class are almost as plentiful in the northernmost part of the Middle Rio Grande province as they are in Tewa Polychrome territory. The typically everted rim hints strongly of a southern influence. Taking everything into consideration it does not appear to be solely an outgrowth of the Sankawi-Tewa Polychrome development. On the other hand it does not, as will be seen later, exactly correspond with the normal form for the Middle Rio Grande, except for the rim and at times a somewhat globular shape. It is very possibly a composite not fully standardized, partaking of certain features derived from both areas. Another point which cannot be determined at present is whether the polished red base of Tewa Polychrome was inspired by Posuge Red or vice versa. Very few bowl fragments showing a corresponding all-over polished treatment have turned up on strictly Tewa Polychrome sites. Some emphasis has been given the type just discussed as it vitally affects the later trends of Upper Rio Grande ceramic development.

The designation chosen for this pottery type is derived from the Tewa place-name for a locality which appropriately lies about midway between the Upper and Middle Rio Grande provinces.

It may be seen that a merging of the two types took place at a later date, sometime between the beginning and the middle of the 18th Century, which resulted in the genesis of three new types: a somewhat altered form of Tewa Polychrome, which may be called Ogapoge Polychrome; another that was definitely a hybrid resulting from a mixture of the Posuge and Tewa types, Pojoaque Polychrome; and a polished black variety, Kapo Black.

OGAPOGE POLYCHROME

Taken in the above order, the first to be brought to attention is one in which certain changes have taken place that serve to differentiate this derivative of Tewa Polychrome from the parent form. Although the general shape remained the same as that of its prototype including the typically tall neck, this latter feature is now found terminating in a flaring rim, apparently taken over from the Posuge side of its ancestry.

A curious case of what appears to be a degeneration in decorative treatment also occurring at this time is seen in the perfunctorily applied red zone that encircles the jar just beneath the lowest band of decoration. This ring appears to be a vestige of and a concession to the custom which formerly, in the preceding Tewa Polychrome, had decreed a solid red base. It is worthy of note that this substitution has consistently persisted on into the 20th Century.

Quite a number of new and interesting ideas with regard to the character and scope of design are manifest in this period. One of the most decided reversals of former usage was the full utilization of olla necks, as a field for decoration, hitherto left blank except for a narrow space on the rim immediately below the lip. Although the neck began to receive attention, yet, with characteristic conservatism, the usual decorative band encircling the vessel at its greatest circumference was, in most cases, retained as a separate feature, more frequently with little relation to the character of the neck design above it. Another change may be seen in the marked coarsening of the elements used in design structure. Heavy lines and an increase in the size of solid masses became the fashion. Still another innovation was the incorporation of a red pigment of an inorganic nature as an integral part of painted design and, lastly, it was during the life of this type that influences in design originating in the Hopi region but largely coming by way of the Little Colorado province began to be felt. A more detailed account of this influence will appear later on in a special section devoted to the subject of an eastward spread of certain motifs of known western derivation. Examples are shown on plates XVI, XVIII and XIX.

When the necessity arises, the name Ogapoge Polychrome will be used to distinguish this type from the earlier Tewa Polychrome, as well as from the better known later developments which include a number of styles appearing after each of the several villages began to specialize in its own distinctive system of design. The period in which these later individualistic styles first appear is believed to have begun about the middle of the 19th Century.

Ogapoge is a Tewa term for the locality now occupied by the city of Santa Fé.

POJOAQUE POLYCHROME

Another type of water jar, previously mentioned as possessing all the characteristics of a hybrid, combined the polished red neck taken from Posuge Red with a typically placed decorative zone, comprised of black designs on a cream colored slip, derived from Tewa Polychrome. While the idea of the band closely follows Tewa usage, there is a noticeable simplification of design, usually rather coarsely executed after the manner of the times. The basal portion of this type also shows the substitution of a red band, as just described for Ogapoge Polychrome, for the earlier all-over treatment. Besides typical examples shown on plates XXI, XXII and XXIII another has been used for the frontispiece in Kidder and Amsden's *Pottery of Pecos*.[6] For purposes of reference this type may be called Pojoaque Polychrome, which refers to an abandoned Indian pueblo in which sherds of this type occur.

KAPO BLACK

The third variety to which attention is now directed, ranges in color from dense black to a very dark shade of gray, the latter possibly at times resulting from a lack of experience in the handling of an unfamiliar process. Though it is also quite as likely that some of the lighter shades have followed an attempt to produce the desired effect without first applying an adequate slip, preliminary slipping appears to have given the most satisfactory results. This latter explanation seems to be borne out because in vessels possessing a good black, that color is seen to extend down onto the lower portion of the jar to a distance equaling the width of the usual red basal ring described for the two preceding types, the balance of the base having a more grayish cast. The slip employed was the ordinary red slip of Posuge Red, dark colors not appearing until, by a method of smudging, a deposition of carbon had taken place. Guthe,[7] in his book on Pueblo pottery manufacture, gives a detailed account of the technique.

As regards the first appearance of this exterior smudging, a time not much

---

[6] Kidder and Amsden, 1931, frontispiece.
[7] Guthe, 1935, p. 74.

earlier than the very end of the 17th Century must be assumed, as polished black sherds are exceedingly scarce in any of the sites known to have been temporarily occupied during the period from 1680 to 1694.

Instead of being an independent invention as might at first be suspected, this treatment appears to be merely a new and refined use of a method possessing a considerable antiquity in the Southwest. Originating as a finish applied to the interior of bowls some time before the 12th Century, usage seems to have been more or less continuous on the interiors of utility wares in both the lower and middle Rio Grande regions until the beginning of the 18th Century. Many of the sites in the latter area, inhabited during the last part of that period, yield a large percentage of sherds with interior surfaces burnished and blackened. Thus, given a wide-spread understanding of the process, it was only natural that in course of time someone would experiment with such a finish for exterior application.

Olla shapes, in all particulars, are the same as those of the two other cognate members in this group, Ogapoge and Pojoaque Polychromes. This tall necked type may appropriately be called Kapo Black, from Kapo, the native name for the pueblo of Santa Clara where smudging has been and is still a predominant practice. Two examples are illustrated on plates XXIV and XXV.

Black pottery, regardless of vessel form, continued in use in most of the Upper Rio Grande villages well into the 20th Century and was the only kind, except culinary wares, known to have been made at the pueblo of Santa Clara until within the last few years. Curiously, the nearby town of San Juan, another pueblo making no pottery with painted decoration, seems to be the only one in this district where the unsmudged polished red treatment has survived, although the black variety was also produced.

In the Middle Rio Grande area however, one other pueblo, Isleta, is known to have made nothing but undecorated polished red pottery, at least since its re-founding sometime between 1709 and 1718, a previous settlement somewhere in the same neighborhood having been abandoned following the Pueblo uprising of 1680. Authority for such a statement rests on a thorough study of sectioned refuse deposits in the present village conducted by staff members of the Laboratory of Anthropology.

On the other hand, decorated red pottery with designs in black organic paint was made to a limited extent in several of the pueblos in both the Upper and Middle Rio Grande provinces, from the latter part of 19th Century on into the 20th. But as all examples so far seen exhibit both late shapes and a form of decoration known to have been in use after village specializations had taken place, these may be largely dismissed as apart from the present subject. Specimens of this type can be cited from the pueblos of San Ildefonso and Tesuque in the Upper Rio Grande and from Cochiti and Santo Domingo in the neighboring district to the south.

Sometime after the middle of the 18th Century tall necked olla shapes began to be generally replaced by the more globular forms with proportionally shorter necks, more like those of the Middle Rio Grande to the south, except in the village of Santa Clara where elongate necks, though in a greatly constricted form, were retained.

From evidence furnished by sherds and a few water jars obtained at temporarily occupied refugee sites in northern New Mexico, Ogapoge Polychrome and Pojoaque Polychrome were then at the height of their development. Stallings[8] has secured dates from beams found in a number of these sites which show that buildings were being erected in this region between the years of 1730 and 1750 +. Two examples of Ogapoge Polychrome and one of Pojoaque Polychrome which were unearthed by E. H. Morris[9] at a ruin in Gobernador Cañon are shown on plates XVI, XVII and XXI. A date for this site was secured by Stallings which indicates an occupation shortly after 1750.

Bowl forms associated with all three of the olla types follow the Tewa formula in having upright rims distinct from the vessel's curve and are found with exterior finishes of polychrome, polished red, and black (plates XX and XXVI).

THE MIDDLE RIO GRANDE CERAMIC PROVINCE

Having now followed the developments of the several pottery types belonging to the Upper Rio Grande province, up to a time when the better known styles of today began to evolve, the same course will be pursued for the Middle Rio Grande province.

The change from the depressed olla forms of the 16th Century to taller shapes in this district was not marked by any single definite developmental stage. What took place can best be described as an intergradation of local shapes with those of the Upper Rio Grande, though there was a general emphasis placed on globular outlines.

Glaze-paint decoration, resulting from the use of an inorganic paint, became one of the principal characteristics of the Middle Rio Grande. It first appeared in the 14th Century but ran a much less extended course than did the organic matte pigments of the neighboring territory to the north. Paints capable of producing a glaze or having a mineral constituent were discontinued not very long after the opening of the 18th Century, except in the villages of Tsia and Santa Ana, having been superseded in all others by the northern organic kind. In these two pueblos, following the passing of glaze decoration, a pigment containing a mineral substance has continued to be employed although the ability or desire to produce a glaze has been lost for nearly two hundred years.

Again, an explanation of the evolutionary changes with regard to shape which took place in this province though otherwise comparatively uniform for the area as a whole, becomes complicated by the fact that these same two villages were subjected to an additional outside influence beyond that of the rest of the district, one emanating from a western source. This divergence will be dealt with after the more general features have been discussed.

---

[8] Stallings, 1938, p. 3. L.A. 1063, 1687, 1684, 1868, 1869, 1871, 1872.
[9] Unpublished.

KOTYITI GLAZE-POLYCHROME

The move, which resulted in the substitution of taller olla forms for the squat round bottomed sort, seems to have taken place quite rapidly and at a comparatively late date. This is borne out by the few evidences of the former to be found that can be safely attributed to a time greatly antedating the Pueblo Rebellion of 1680. In those of the earlier class the upper and lower portions of the body meet at such an angle that a very definite carina is formed, the whole being surmounted by a rather short neck with a slightly flaring rim (plates IV and V), while the later shapes are much taller in proportion to the width, and have, in the main, a tendency to be more globular in outline and possess rims usually showing a little more flare (plates XXX and XXXI). Not only did the new fashion decree a considerable increase of the height to width ratio but equally interesting to note is the adoption of the concave bottom, long a standard feature in Tewa Polychrome territory adjacent on the north. As a matter of fact, the whole idea back of this marked change in form may unquestionably be traced to that source though there was a very evident lack of standardization in the resulting forms. Examples can even be cited showing but slightly altered Tewa Polychrome shapes recovered from Middle Rio Grande sites with typical Middle Rio Grande designs in glaze paint. One of these is shown on plate XXXV.

The typical system of decoration in this province called for two distinct and unrelated bands of design, usually of a simple geometric character, executed with glaze paint in combination with inserts of a matte red pigment, on a surface slipped with varying shades of tan, red or white. One of these bands encircled the body of the jar, the other being confined to the neck. For a detailed study of glaze-paint decoration, the reader is referred to Kidder's[10] analysis of design.

In regard to the succession of bowl shapes quite a different state of affairs existed, as there was apparently but little direct correlation with the evolution of olla forms. Beginning with the direct unspecialized rims of the 14th Century which conformed to the curvature of the bowl, a number of progressive modifications involving a thickening of this feature took place during the succeeding years[11] until by the beginning of the 16th Century this process of reinforcement had reached its greatest proportions (plate VI). Following this thickened rim type came another much thinner, placed upright at an obtuse angle with the vessel's curve (plates XXXVI and XXXVII). It is important to note that this latest change was not made at the same time that ollas became taller but occurred at somewhat earlier date, early enough to have been the style which inspired like forms occasionally appearing, as previously noted, in the Upper Rio Grande province in Sankawi Black-on-cream sites and which afterward became the normal type for Tewa Polychrome and its immediate successors.

Bowls were decorated both within and without, and present no notable stylistic differences in design from the sort used on jars.

[10] Kidder and Shepard, 1936.
[11] Mera, 1932. Kidder and Shepard, 1936.

Usually a more or less polished slip or wash, dull red in color as a rule, covered the entire basal portion of both bowls and ollas, though examples of the latter have been noted which were evidently made late enough to have been influenced by that northern custom in which entire slipping gave place to a narrow zone of red, applied just beneath the lower band of design.

The term Kotyiti Polychrome[12] has been previously applied to the latest bowl form with a glaze-paint decoration and could also with excellent reason be used to include the class of tall water jars with concave bottoms, as both represent the final development in shape upon which that kind of paint was used, despite the fact that the former first appears at a somewhat earlier date than do the ollas. Kotyiti is the Keres name for a village which has yielded much material illustrative of the type.

Previously attention has been called to the eventual substitution of a matte paint for the glaze sort, earlier a determinant of the ceramics in this province, as demonstrating a strong influence from the north. On the other hand, although northern long necked shapes for a time also exerted quite a little influence on the more spherical indigenous forms, the latter in the end gained the ascendency and finally, with some modification, practically superseded all others over the entire Pueblo region, though not altogether accepted in every part until well into the 19th Century.

PUNAME POLYCHROME

Referring back to the villages of Tsia and Santa Ana, the only ones in this province to continue the use of a mineral paint, another difference is found in the presence of olla shapes having certain features unlike any others heretofore described. This new form will be more understandable after the Little Colorado province has been discussed, as it was in part inspired from styles peculiar to that region. For the present it is only necessary to say that the most characteristic feature of this type is a neck that has been reduced to nearly vestigial proportions. Three of these are illustrated on plates XXXVIII, XXXIX and LX, the first of which was obtained at a temporarily occupied site proven to have been inhabited for some time after 1750. This alien influence did not affect the styles in the western part of the Middle Rio Grande territory until well after the beginning of the 18th Century, in which section there were also, as might be expected, a number of shapes that show intergradations between the new type and both the northern long necked and more globular sorts (plates XXXVIII, XLI, XLII and XLIII). These hybrid shapes appear to have finally lost favor between the middle and end of the 19th Century. Further attention will be given this somewhat heterogeneous group of olla forms under the section devoted to design as it is also directly connected with that subject. The name Puname Polychrome is proposed as a designation for vessels of this type, as Puname was applied by some of the early explorers to the inhabitants of the district in which the pueblos of Tsia and Santa Ana are now situated.

[12] Mera, 1933, p. 9.

THE LITTLE COLORADO CERAMIC PROVINCE

For this district, the best evidence concerning the types of early historic pottery has resulted from Hodge's[13] excavations at Hawikuh, a Zuñi village abandoned about 1670. Stratification tests made during the work indicated that when the Spanish first made their appearance in 1540, two distinct types of pottery were in use; one, rapidly going into a decline; the other, a revival of an older technique, again coming into popularity. The first of these was a matte-paint polychrome ware which seems to have been an attempt to copy Hopi styles but through lack of the proper kind of clay the makers were forced to use a buff slip in order to imitate as closely as possible the yellow and orange tones of Hopi wares. But rivaling this in popularity was an incoming pottery type on which is seen the revival of glaze-paint decoration, an art previously practiced in this area for a number of centuries before the attempt was made to imitate Hopi fashions. In fact it seems quite possible that in the eastern part of the province glaze pigments were never entirely discarded, as a study of a good series of sherds from deep refuse deposits at Acoma brought to light an almost negligible percentage of matte-paint specimens.

As nothing but sherds of the matte-paint ware have been available for study and also as this type appears to be more intimately connected with the subject of Hopi styles, concerning which too little is known at present, no detailed discussion at this time is possible beyond stating that depressed, round bottomed olla forms seem to have prevailed.

HAWIKUH POLYCHROME

These same characteristics were typical of the shapes of the incoming glaze-paint type.

Despite the fact that a similar glaze medium was also used for the purposes of decoration in the Middle Rio Grande district, ollas of this new type, other than a common use of glaze paint and a mutual resemblance in proportionate height and rounding bases, differed radically in shape from any common to the eastern area. Some of the distinguishing features of this style are called to attention in the following brief description. But before beginning, the reader is advised to consult the cross section shown on plate XLVII in order to gain a better understanding of the text. It will be noticed that from a point a short distance above the widest part of the body there begins a gentle upward and inward slope, slightly concave in outline, which forms the comparatively short neck. There is little if any break shown in the profile to differentiate one from the other. Necks normally terminated in a peculiar thickening of the rim which projects in a narrow flange on the exterior to form a lip. A very slight concavity serves to distinguish the upper from the basal portions of jars. Additional examples are illustrated on plates XLVIII, XLIX, L and LI.

Bowl rims have a pronounced incurve and are provided with the same type of

---

[13] Hodge, 1923, p. 29.

reinforced lips as those used on jars, though sometimes their bottoms were flattened instead of having been rounded (plates LII and LIII).

On ollas, the typical system of decoration, as in the Middle Rio Grande district, called for two bands of design, one encircling the periphery and another placed just below the rim, though exceptions to this rule may be seen. Bowls have a single band on the exterior but unlike those of the area to the east, interior decoration does not commonly appear on true Little Colorado forms of this period, although in the following stage of development there was a complete reversal of this custom. The name Hawikuh Polychrome might appropriately be retained for this type because the greatest amount of information concerning the styles of the early part of the historic period has been obtained from the ruin bearing that name.

Evidence furnished by sherds, indicates that this style persisted at least up to the time of the Pueblo Rebellion in 1680. In that uprising the remaining Zuñi villages, then five in number, together with Acoma in the eastern part of the province, are known to have taken an active part and from that time on there is a history of unsettled conditions continuing until well into the first part of the 18th Century. By the year 1705 the survivors of the several Zuñi pueblos had been gathered into the single community which now bears that name.

ASHIWI POLYCHROME

About the time that a partial stabilization of social conditions had been effected, a vogue for taller olla shapes with concave bottoms was introduced from the east. In support of this statement, it can be pointed out that sherds of this later type have not been found at any of the six villages which preceded the founding of the present town of Zuñi, from which a few entire vessels in a good state of preservation have been recovered. Although no exact time can be given for this change in fashion, it is known to have taken place while glaze paint was to a limited extent still in use (plate LIV). This medium, however, seems to have been very shortly given up in favor of an organic matte paint which appears with few exceptions, to have accompanied the adoption of taller shapes.

As might be expected, the change in height to width ratio was not accomplished without the retention for a while of certain features belonging to the preceding type; so much is this the case that the earlier shapes can be considered as modifications of a basic form rather than anything resembling direct copies of eastern styles.

The most striking departure from earlier usage consists in the adoption of a concave depression in the base and the substitution of a strongly convex treatment of the neck for one that was slightly concave, which gives to that part of the jar a somewhat dome-like outline (plates LV, LVI and LVIII). Because this represents such a distinct stage in the line of evolution, jars having convex necks, without regard to character of paint, could appropriately be called Ashiwi Polychrome to distinguish them from the later locally specialized developments now known as Acoma and Zuñi Polychromes. The name Ashiwi is the Zuñian tribal designation.

For a while the typical thickening of the lip was retained but afterward this became thin and direct. Convexly curved necks with more or less reinforced rims are known to have survived until as late as the middle of the 18th Century. About this same time rims began to lose their thickness and were turned up to form a short neck so that that part of the vessel which was originally a convex neck became instead the upper portion of the body (plates LX to LXII). It was from this source that the two westernmost Middle Rio Grande towns, Tsia and Santa Ana, derived their short necked olla shapes (plates XXXVIII to XLV). About the middle of the 19th Century these Ashiwi forms seem to have already become largely merged with the shapes of today.

No radical changes like those marking the development of Ashiwi Polychrome jars are to be found affecting the bowl shapes of this period, the principal difference lying in the substitution of a simple direct rim for the thickened sort. Both flat and round bottomed forms occur (plates LXV and LXVI).

Slipping the entire basal portions of both bowls and jars with red or brown was and still remains the accepted practice. So firmly has this custom been established in this particular province that the writer has seen but a single example out of the many hundreds examined where this treatment has been reduced to the narrow zone which is a characteristic procedure for the later styles in both the Upper and Middle Rio Grande provinces.

There was a decided tendency to break away from the traditional decorative system which called for two distinct and usually unrelated bands of design, probably because of the change in vessel forms which provided a field for decoration differing considerably in size and shape. Nevertheless, some use of these formal divisions was made until about the middle of the 18th Century, after which time the more generalized globular shapes then coming into favor made an all-over design treatment more practical and pleasing.

No attempt has been made to enter into any descriptions involving the numerous minor variations of both shape and decoration which help to distinguish the work of one village from that of others. To do so at this time would only tend to obscure the broader aspects of a general evolutionary development.

THE HOPI CERAMIC PROVINCE

It is a matter of considerable regret that the styles native to this province cannot be included at this time but, as before stated, not enough is known about the entire series of developmental steps in this area to warrant a discussion. Despite this dearth of information, it should be of interest to know that finally, here too, taller olla shapes were introduced, though the resulting forms are quite distinct from those developed in any of the previously discussed cultural areas. So it may be seen that in the end there was completed an east to west spread of a new idea concerning vessel forms which progressively succeeded in replacing or greatly modifying those of all the older established concepts.

PART II

A TREND IN DECORATION

THE FEATHER MOTIVE IN HISTORIC DESIGN

While the westward spread of a vogue for taller olla forms was taking place, another movement concerned with a certain style of decoration was pursuing a course in exactly the opposite direction, that is, from west to east. Designs of this class, although exhibiting a wide range of variation in structural detail, are all easily identified by the inclusion of a common factor, which appears in the form of conventionalized feather symbols. But before proceeding farther, it should first be explained that the term symbol, as here used, in no way implies any ceremonial significance but is employed merely as a convenient designation for these design units.

The source from which feather forms were derived was a regional decorative development native to the Hopi province. The pottery type upon which this sort of decoration appears to have reached its highest expression is known as Sikyatki Polychrome, which was especially notable for an elaborate treatment of highly abstract bird and feather forms. This general system of design was in use from at least as early as the first part of the 16th Century, as shown by material found in the ruins of Sikyatki,[14] on to as late as the abandonment of that settlement which is believed to have occurred not a great many years before the arrival of the Spanish in 1540. A very similar system was still in use at the time that Awatovi, another town in the Hopi area, was destroyed in 1700. At this point, as a matter of precaution, it may be well to make it clear that the bird designs mentioned above should in no way be confused with those simple hook-like symbols first appearing in much earlier black-on-white pottery times and which continued to be used to some extent during a number of later developments. Plates V, VII and XXXVI illustrate a late use of this symbol.

Sikyatki designs, with an especial emphasis on feather forms, exerted a very strong influence on the styles of the neighboring Little Colorado district, sometimes to such an extent that what appear to be direct copies were attempted (plate LI). Usually however, the features taken from the Hopi system were combined with those of the indigenous variety thus producing a distinct type of decoration. One serious drawback encountered in making these adaptations, both in the Little Colorado and Middle Rio Grande provinces, resulted from the use of glaze paint. This was apparently a difficult medium to control and had plainly hampered the artist in attempts to reproduce the fine lines and other refinements characteristic of Hopi

---

[14] Fewkes, 1898, 1898a, 1919.

25

work. Tending to substantiate such a view is the very noticeable technical advance in draftsmanship and added complexity of the patterns coming into use after the introduction of matte pigments.

On plate LXVII a few of the more common Sikyatki bird and feather forms are shown, some of which, for the sake of clarity, have been drawn detached from the elaborations of which they were a part. These illustrate a few of the basic forms from which later adaptations in other regions were derived.

In the Little Colorado province designs featuring feather symbols became extremely popular from late glaze times on into the era of matte-paint decoration, at which time a considerable degree of structural complexity was achieved. Plates LII and LIII illustrate examples designed during the glaze-paint era while plates LV and LX show others executed in the later matte-paint period. But eventually these last in turn seem to have been largely discarded sometime toward the end of the 18th Century. This change is believed to have occurred when stiffly formal patterns were beginning to be replaced by others having a greater degree of freedom in rendition, styles which were closely akin to some of those in use today.

In tracing an eastward extension of the use of the feather motif, it will be first necessary to revert to the subject of olla shapes as both of these features were equally involved in the movement. More specifically, the shapes to which reference is now made have been previously noted as occurring exclusively in the villages of Tsia and Santa Ana (plates XXXVIII to XLV). This particular style includes adaptations of some of the later Little Colorado forms with convexly arched necks, after thickened lips had given place to upright rudimentary necks. This statement appears to be borne out by the fact that no evidence has been secured, from either intact vessels or sherds, to indicate that the thick lipped type was ever imitated in those settlements. A good example coming from a short-lived site occupied about the middle of the 18th Century is figured on the first of the above plates which shows that by that time the style for extremely short necks, in some instances hardly distinguishable from rims, had become fully established.

Arriving simultaneously with the new jar form came certain features of Little Colorado decoration, among which feathers may be seen to occupy a prominent position. While a number of these design units were accepted in principle, nearly all were modified to harmonize with the already established ideas on decoration (plates XXXVIII, XLI, XLII and XLV). It is an interesting point to note that ever since the introduction of western styles into the Middle Rio Grande area, there are, in many respects, close resemblances in the character of design in both the villages of Tsia and Acoma, in the Little Colorado district. Some of these similarities have even persisted to the present time and on pottery from both areas feather derivatives occasionally may be found incorporated in the designs on vessels of the very latest modes. In fact there exists a closer affinity in decorative styles between these two towns than can be found among any of the others in the entire Pueblo region. Such evidence appears to provide additional confirmation for the stand taken in grouping the short necked olla forms of Tsia and Santa Ana, irrespective of minor variations in shape and differences of design, under the term Puname Polychrome.

From here, a further extension of certain features of western style may be traced into both the eastern part of the Middle Rio Grande province and northward into the adjacent Upper Rio Grande, but in this instance it was of design alone. It may be recalled that about the middle of the 18th Century, the pottery of both these areas had begun to have a great deal in common, due to the adoption in the lower district of Upper Rio Grande types of slip, matte paint and often of design as well. Hence, due to such similarities, it has been found practically impossible to differentiate the work of one province from that of the other between that time and the beginning of the period of individual village specializations.

In decorative compositions traceable to a western influence, feather forms were used principally as appendages to elaborate a type of design in which attempts were being made to break away from an inherited and stiffly formal system (plates XVII, XVIII and XIX). Although designs of this class attained quite a high degree of popularity for a time, their vogue does not appear to have continued much beyond the first part of the 19th Century, gradually giving place to designs very similar to those now in use.

Nevertheless, even though feather symbolism itself failed to survive there can be little doubt but that the complex and freely executed designs from the west were, in the main, largely responsible for the final disappearance of the more elemental and formalized eastern forms.

Thus it may be seen that while a fancy for higher olla shapes was taking a westward course from the place of origin in northeastern Pueblo territory, an influence, which profoundly affected the future of ceramic designing, was making its way in the opposite direction.

The length of time taken by the fashion for tall concave-bottomed vessels to traverse the entire Pueblo region appears to have been approximately a hundred and fifty years, the first century of which went by before these forms began to appear to any extent south of an arbitrary line separating the Upper from the Middle Rio Grande province. After this, however, the spread was comparatively rapid. The eastward course of design, on the other hand, does not appear to have made much headway until after the arrival of tall shapes in the west, sometime in the first quarter of the 18th Century.

The reason for such radical changes in style is of course purely conjectural. It is hard to believe that any particular stimulus can be credited directly to the Spanish who harassed and oppressed the aboriginal population to a high degree, unless they perhaps unwittingly furnished a means of dissemination through contacts made in concentration camps of the *encomienda* system. Such contacts may, within reason, be held to have been responsible in part for the building up of that solidarity of purpose among the peoples of several linguistic stocks and dialects which resulted in the great Pueblo Rebellion of 1680, and which as well could have provided an opportunity for an exchange of ideas concerning other matters, including the question of style. There seems to be some basis for such an hypothesis, as the latter part of the 17th Century and the early years of the 18th were included in the period during which the most striking changes in shape and decoration were taking place.

All this furnishes an interesting commentary on diffusion of style, one which may perhaps prove of value in estimating similar movements in prehistoric times.

While the foregoing presents an account of the broader aspects of this study, more attention will be paid to detail in the remarks accompanying the several illustrations. By following this method, it will be possible to fit each example figured into the pattern outlined in the text.

BIBLIOGRAPHY

BARBOUR, RUTH

1932   Indian labor in the Spanish Colonies. *New Mexico Historical Review*, Vol. VII, Nos. 2, 3 and 4. Albuquerque, 1932.

CHAPMAN, K. M.

1927   A feather symbol of the ancient pueblos. *El Palacio*, Vol. XXIII, No. 21. Santa Fé, 1927.

FEWKES, J. W.

1898   Archaeological expedition to Arizona in 1895. *Seventeenth Annual Report of the Bureau of American Ethnology*, Part 2, pp. 519-742. Washington, 1898.

1898 a   The feather symbol in ancient Hopi designs. *American Anthropologist*, Vol. 11, No. 1, pp. 1-14. Washington, 1898.

1919   Designs on prehistoric Hopi pottery. *Thirty-third Annual Report of the Bureau of American Ethnology*, pp. 207-284. Washington, 1919.

GUTHE, C. E.

1925   Pueblo pottery making, a study at the village of San Ildefonso. *Papers of the Phillips Academy Southwestern Expedition*, No. 2. New Haven, 1925.

HODGE, F. W.

1923   Circular kivas near Hawikuh, New Mexico. *Contributions from the Museum of the American Indian, Heye Foundation*, Vol. VII, No. 1. New York, 1923.

KIDDER, A. V. and C. A. AMSDEN

1931   The pottery of Pecos, Vol. I. The dull-paint wares. *Papers of the Phillips Academy Southwestern Expedition*, No. 5. New Haven, 1931.

KIDDER, A. V. and A. O. SHEPARD

1936   The pottery of Pecos, Vol. II. The glaze-paint, culinary and other wares. *Papers of the Phillips Academy Southwestern Expedition*, No. 7. New Haven, 1936.

MERA, H. P.

1932   Wares ancestral to Tewa Polychrome. *Laboratory of Anthropology, Technical Series*, Bulletin No. 4. Santa Fé, 1932.

1933   A proposed revision of the Rio Grande glaze-paint sequence. *Laboratory of Anthropology, Technical Series*, Bulletin No. 5. Santa Fé, 1933.

1934   A survey of the Biscuit ware area in northern New Mexico. *Laboratory of Anthropology, Technical Series*, Bulletin No. 6. Santa Fé, 1934.

1937   The Rain Bird, a study in Pueblo design. *Memoirs of the Laboratory of Anthropology*, Vol. II. Santa Fé, 1937.

STALLINGS, W. S., JR.

1933   A tree-ring chronology for the Rio Grande drainage in northern New Mexico. *Proceedings of the National Academy of Science*, Vol. 19, No. 9, pp. 803-806. Washington, 1933.

1938   Southwestern dated ruins: I. *Tree-ring Bulletin*, Vol. 4, No. 2, p. 3. Tucson, 1938.

AN EXPLANATION OF THE PLATES

The following plates have been planned to illustrate both the characteristics of shape as well as the types of design, outlined in the preceding text. Each includes a half-tone cut which gives some idea of the gross appearance of the vessel, but has perhaps a greater value in showing the placement of design. The accompanying cross section reveals the entire contour in such a manner that comparisons may be the more easily made. Lastly as an aid to a clearer understanding of composition and structure of design, a more or less diagramatic representation of the zone or zones of decoration is included on each plate. These have been executed uniformly, without attempting to reproduce any of the various original colors or shades.

Concerning this latter feature, it is well to explain at the outset that it is manifestly impossible to reproduce, in anything like their exact proportions, the several parts of a design when transferred from a curved to a plane surface. As a consequence, the draftsman has been confronted by a difficult problem, one which involved the making of certain adjustments to compensate for such changes; but wherever these allowances have had to be made there has been kept constantly in mind the preservation of as close a likeness to the appearance of the original as possible.

Furthermore, in many instances the pigments, especially the glazes, have run or smeared so badly during the process of firing or from other causes that patterns have become greatly obscured. Therefore, all runs and other evidences of poor workmanship have been ignored in these adaptations, the better to make clear the intent of the decorator.

Unless otherwise noted drawings for the plates are by the author, the photographs by the Laboratory of Anthropology.

PLATE I

Biscuit Ware Olla†

Form: This plate illustrates a typically depressed, round bottomed water jar of late prehistoric age from the Upper Rio Grande region. The short neck seen here was a concomitant of this style, in this instance showing a slightly outward flaring toward the rim.

Decoration: Black matte paint on a grayish ground with a tan undertone.

Painted designs on Biscuit ware ollas were, with few exceptions, restricted to a single band, usually divided into panels, applied just above the greatest circumference. On this example may be seen a fingered symbol termed an *awanyu*. There is a wide difference of opinion as to what it represents: a plumed serpent, the guardian spirit of springs and water courses; growing maize; or a highly conventionalized hand. Those *awanyus* in the first and fourth panels possess seven digits each, while the remainder have only six.

The band of decoration is nowhere interrupted by a ceremonial break,* a feature more frequently present in later developments.

† Since this paper was written Dr. A. V. Kidder has named the type shown herein Bandelier Black-on-gray (Kidder and Shepard, 1936, p. xxx).

* "Ceremonial break," a term frequently applied to an intentional gap left in the framing lines or other parts of pottery designs, is an inexact usage inasmuch as it implies a direct connection with a rite or ceremony. On the contrary, such breaks appear to be merely visible manifestations concerned with some form of belief. It has been retained here because, through long continued use, that designation would be most widely recognized.

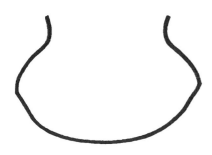

PLATE II

Biscuit Ware Olla

Form: The olla shown opposite conforms to the prevailing fashion of the times, only slightly differing from the specimen on plate I by reason of a more direct neck.

Decoration: Black matte paint on a lightly gray ground.

The decorative scheme departs from the more usual in two ways. There is no division of the band of design into panels and a series of four figures in outline, which may represent bird forms, have been drawn at intervals on the underbody.

No ceremonial break has been made in the band of decoration.

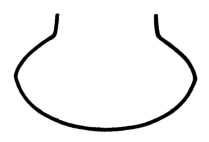

PLATE II
Biscuit Ware Olla
Height 9 inches
Indian Arts Fund, 87

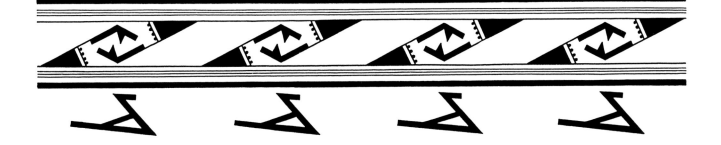

PLATE III

Biscuit Ware Bowl

Form: Bowls with more or less rounded bottoms were the vogue during this ceramic period. Note the specialized and thickened rim.

Decoration: Black matte paint on a gray ground.

The exterior zone of decoration has been separated into four panels, one of which, probably due to a miscalculation, is much shorter than the others. Despite this, the same design units were adapted to the different spacing.

Two *awanyus* are incorporated in the decoration on the interior of the bowl. These have only four digits as compared with a greater number for those shown on plate I.

An unusual occurrence in Biscuit ware is to be seen in the ceremonial break in the uppermost framing line, the rest of the band being unaffected.

PLATE III
Biscuit Ware Bowl
Diameter 13 inches
Laboratory of Anthropology, 30/1244

PLATE IV

RIO GRANDE GLAZE-POLYCHROME OLLA

Form: Rounded bottoms, short necks and median, circumferentially placed carinas were normal to ollas of late prehistoric times in the Middle Rio Grande district. The short neck usually terminated in a slightly everted lip, caused partially by an interior beveling of the rim, although on the other hand, there was sometimes also an obvious tendency towards an actual flare.

Decoration: Black glaze and matte red paints on a polished ocher upperbody, dull red beneath.

In the later forms of this ware the application of two distinct bands of decoration on water jars was a fundamental procedure, these bands being usually divided into panels. It may be of interest to note the similarity between the pendant units within the long panels of both upper and lower bands on the specimen here pictured and those used on a Biscuit ware vessel on plate II.

A break in the bottom framing line of the lower band appears to have been accidental.

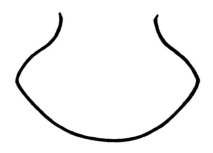

PLATE IV
Rio Grande Glaze-polychrome
Olla
Height 9 inches
Laboratory of Anthropology, 30/1257

PLATE V

Rio Grande Glaze-polychrome Olla

Form: This example displays no deviation from the normal.

Decoration: Dark brown glaze and matte red paints on a light creamy tan, underbody dull red.

Balanced symmetry was apparently not of especial moment to the artist as irregularities in arrangements of detail very frequently can be detected. In the upper zone, at the bottom of the first panel to the left, there is an extra horizontal line which does not match the arrangement in the third panel. Again, note the discorrespondence between the placing of stepped figures in the second and fourth panels. There appears to have been more of a striving for effect than for exactness.

The angled hook-like units with their appendages, appearing in some of the panels in both upper and lower bands, are generally believed to be highly conventionalized bird symbols.

No ceremonial break in either band of design occurs.

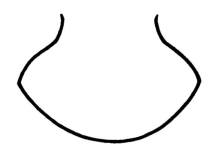

Plate V
Rio Grande Glaze-polychrome
Olla
Height 9½ inches
Laboratory of Anthropology, 30/1256

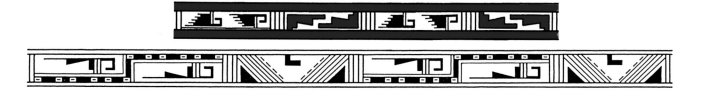

PLATE VI

Rio Grande Glaze-polychrome Bowl

Form: One of the rounded bottom bowl forms of late prehistoric times with the typically thickened rim which probably served to reinforce and strengthen that part.

Decoration: Dark brown glaze and matte red paints on a creamy tan slip.

The designs, both inside and outside, are so elemental that they require little comment. However, that on the interior presents an opening in the ring framing the design which is usually accepted as having had some esoteric significance.

PLATE VI
Rio Grande Glaze-polychrome
Bowl
Diameter 11 inches
Laboratory of Anthropology, 30/43

PLATE VII

Jemez Black-on-white Olla

Form: Ollas representative of this pottery type, although existing on the same time level as Biscuit ware and the glaze-paint pottery of the Middle Rio Grande, have little in common with the depressed jar shapes typical for those wares and agree closely in only one particular, the use of rounded bottoms. Transversely placed handles, rarely found in any other form of late Pueblo pottery, were characteristic for the Jemez type.

Decoration: Gray-black matte paint varying to brownish in places, on an oyster white ground.

The decorative band shows indifferent drawing, organization and spacing and is not continuous about the vessel, being divided by a ceremonial break an inch in width. Two examples of stylized bird forms may be seen on the line above the groups of solid stepped figures. For other variations of this symbol see plates V and XXXVI.

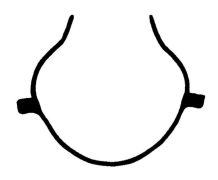

PLATE VII
Jemez Black-on-white Olla
Height 11 inches
Sheldon Parsons collection

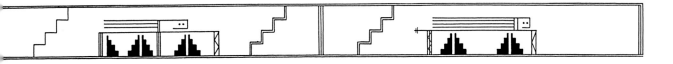

PLATE VIII

Jemez Black-on-white Bowl

Form: The round bottomed bowl shown here is typical for this pottery type. There were, as a rule, few attempts to introduce a specialized rim form although copies of those pertaining to wares from neighboring regions are occasionally found.

Decoration: Gray-black, verging to brownish in places, on an oyster white ground.

The interior decorative treatment shows little effort to obtain a balanced arrangement in design. Exteriorly a more orderly course is pursued, the only deviation being seen in the two hooked figures, probably adaptations of a bird symbol, which replace the serrations otherwise employed.

Ceremonial breaks occur in both inside and outside designs, the latter of which can be found at the base of the hooked unit toward the left.

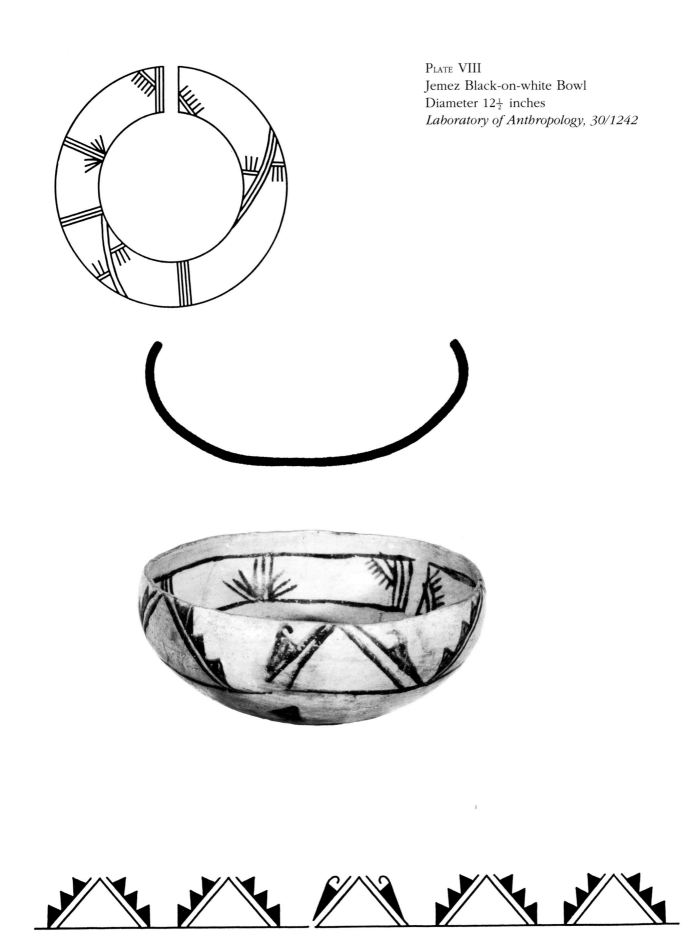

PLATE VIII
Jemez Black-on-white Bowl
Diameter 12½ inches
Laboratory of Anthropology, 30/1242

PLATE IX

Little Colorado Glaze-polychrome Olla

Form: Depressed, round bottomed olla forms also dominated the styles of late prehistoric times in the Little Colorado ceramic province. One of the striking differences between the shapes of this area and those of the Middle Rio Grande region will be noted in the rounded mid-section of the former as opposed to the peripherally located carina of the latter. There is also a slight concavity extending around the vessel just below the bulge that tends to differentiate an upper from a basal section. Compare the cross section of this and those on plates IV and V.

Decoration: Dull brownish black glaze and matte red paints on a creamy white ground.

Particular attention is directed to four horizontally placed design units consisting of two feathers with triangular side appendages which simulate the highly conventionalized rear extremity of a bird. Such units together with feather symbols in general were undoubtedly borrowed from the adjacent Hopi ceramic province. On plate LXVII may be seen similar forms. One of the tail feathers at the left lacks the red coloring applied to all the rest, probably an oversight.

A ceremonial opening breaks the broad red stripe immediately above the band of design but this interruption does not extend to any other part of the decorative zone nor to the serrated band about the rim.

48

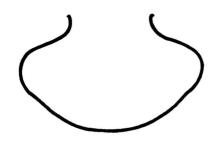

PLATE IX
Little Colorado Glaze-
polychrome Olla
Height 8½ inches
Indian Arts Fund, 1037

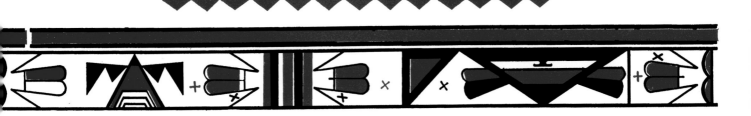

PLATE X

Little Colorado Glaze-polychrome Bowl

Form: As in the preceding member of this ceramic group (plate IX), the bowl here figured also has a shallow concavity separating the rounded basal portion from the strongly convex upper part. The cross section illustrates a highly specialized, thickened lip. Both of these features became characteristic for both bowls and jars during the late styles of glaze-paint decoration and were continued after the introduction of matte pigments.

Decoration: Dark greenish glaze and matte red paints on a creamy white ground.

Although there is a hint of Rio Grande design in the use of stepped or fret units, these are not filled in solidly but have been made less heavy in appearance by the incorporation of open spaces through which the base color is allowed to show. Note the two stylized dragonflies, a symbol, appertaining to water, which is often depicted in this region.

No ceremonial break appears.

PLATE X
Little Colorado Glaze-
polychrome Bowl
Diameter 8½ inches
Indian Arts Fund, 819

PLATE XI

Sankawi Black-on-cream Olla

Form: This pottery type, originating in the Upper Rio Grande province, was the first to show a complete breaking away from depressed jar shapes, the accepted fashion during the later phases of prehistoric Pueblo pottery development. The appearance of this tall necked form with a concave depression in the bottom marked the beginning of radical changes in style for all the Pueblo ceramic provinces existing during the historic era.

Decoration: Black matte paint on a light cream colored ground.

Upon a comparison of this type with that of its predecessor, Biscuit ware (plates I, II and III), it is quite evident that the quality of line work is finer and that solid areas are less extensive.

The *awanyu*, two of which are included in the design here presented, is thus shown to have survived as a unit of decoration. In this case five digits were used, differing in this respect from those previously shown on plates I and III. Note the disparity in length between the body portions of these two symbols.

There are four distinct ceremonial breaks; one dividing the decorative band about the neck, one through the three upper framing lines, another through the four lower framing lines and lastly there is a wide gap in the row of inverted arches at the bottom. None is opposite any other.

52

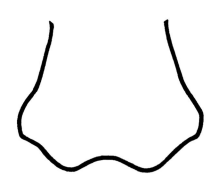

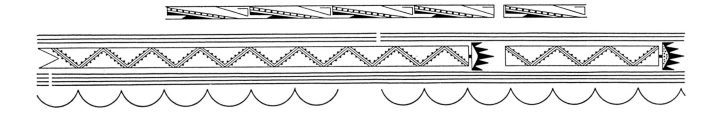

PLATE XII

Sankawi Black-on-cream Olla

Form: No comment is necessary as this specimen varies in no way from the normal.
Decoration: Black matte paint on a light cream colored ground.

The draftsmanship displayed on this jar was of a very poor order. In dividing the zone of decoration into panels, the craftsman miscalculated and was forced to insert a short length of the dotted band in the space next to the panel on the left in order to complete the design. Also, near the center, a triangular space was left open which does not match like areas solidly filled.

No ceremonial break occurs in the row of pendant triangles below the rim nor is there any separation of the main band of decoration but this feature may be represented by an interruption of the zigzag line below.

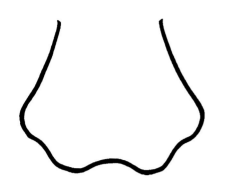

PLATE XII
Sankawi Black-on-cream Olla
Height 12½ inches
Laboratory of Anthropology, 30/64

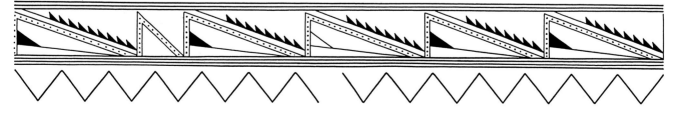

PLATE XIII

Sankawi Black-on-cream Bowl

Form: A round bottomed bowl typical of the Sankawi developmental stage. The specialized rims, so frequently used in Biscuit ware (plate III), appear to have been largely discarded during the life of this pottery type.

Decoration: Black matte paint on a light cream colored ground.

Poor drawing and lack of balance detract from the effectiveness of the designs on this vessel. Though simple in conception and offering no particular difficulties in the way of execution, irregularities in the arrangement and structure of the hatched units on either side of the two vertical lines may be seen toward the left end of the exterior decorative band. The hatched triangular areas in the bowl's interior require no comment.

A ceremonial break affects only the two uppermost framing lines.

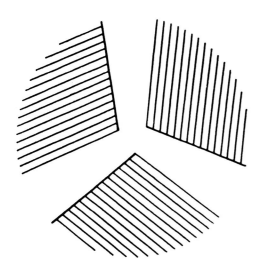

Plate XIII
Sankawi Black-on-cream Bowl
Diameter $10\frac{1}{4}$ inches
Laboratory of Anthropology, 30/1243

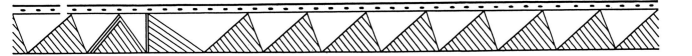

PLATE XIV

Tewa Polychrome Bowl

Form: Although this bowl form has been occasionally noted at Sankawi Black-on-cream villages, in Upper Rio Grande territory, it was not completely adopted as a part of the ceramic complex of that area until the latter part of the 17th Century. Originally this shape was developed in the Middle Rio Grande glaze-paint district. See plates XXXVI and XXXVII.

Decoration: Black matte paint on a creamy white background, with the basal portion of the bowl entirely covered with a well polished red slip. There is no decoration on the interior.

The scheme of design is quite simple but was executed with considerable delicacy and accuracy of line. Note minor differences of design treatment in the several panels. This appears to have been done with the idea of purposely creating variations rather than through a forgetfulness of the character of units employed in the other panels.

No ceremonial break occurs.

This specimen was unearthed at Astialakwa, a village visited by De Vargas in 1693, which was attacked and razed the following year.

PLATE XIV
Tewa Polychrome Bowl
Diameter 11½ inches
Indian Arts Fund, 1594

PLATE XV

Tewa Polychrome Olla

Form: This is the largest fragment of this pottery type, representative of water jars, yet secured. It will be seen that the shape closely follows that of the Sankawi tradition. Reconstruction of the upper part, indicated by thinner lines, has been made possible by evidence secured from a series of neck sherds of the period.

Decoration: Black matte paint on a creamy white ground, basal portion solid red.

Fine lines and well controlled drawing, a criterion for the type, are self evident. The curved elements, more than usually abundant on this example show the beginnings of a tendency to a lesser degree of formalization in design, which becomes more obvious in the next developmental stage.

A ceremonial break was omitted.

Coming from the same ruin as did the one illustrated on the previous plate, it also can be safely dated not later than 1694. Many sherds of this type, agreeing in all particulars, are to be found on Black Mesa adjacent to San Ildefonso where the inhabitants of that pueblo sustained a siege of seven months in 1694.

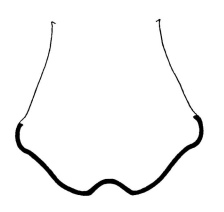

Plate XV
Tewa Polychrome Olla
Diameter $12\frac{1}{4}$ inches
Indian Arts Fund, 827

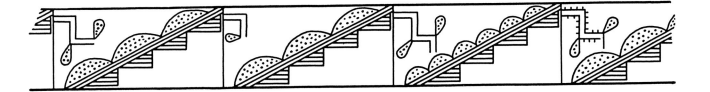

PLATE XVI

Ogapoge Polychrome Olla

Form: Ollas, at this stage of development, although closely resembling both of their ancestral types, Sankawi and Tewa, in body shape and elongate neck, demonstrate a radical change in rim forms which have become distinctly flared. As explained in the text (p. 13) this feature was derived from a ceramic type, Posuge Red, which appears during the life of Tewa Polychrome. Unfortunately, the Posuge type is known only from sherds, a large number of which nevertheless have been available for examination in regard to rim form.

Decoration: Black matte paint on a creamy white ground.

During this stage the neck for the first time is fully utilized as a field for decoration although the sterotyped band of design around the periphery of the vessel is usually retained as well.

It is interesting to observe in the present instance that while the peripheral band exhibits a large measure of the old formality of design, the pattern on the neck shows considerably more freedom of thought, albeit somewhat overdone. Another feature deserving especial attention is to be seen in the feather symbols appended to the paired stepped lines on the neck, an imported feature of design from the west (Little Colorado and Hopi) which begins to appear at this time.

In this type there also first occurs the change by which a comparatively narrow zone of red slip below the peripheral design band is substituted for a fully covered base of that color.

The cut shows what appears to be a ceremonial break in the line separating the neck design from the one beneath which seems to have been overlooked in the drawing.

This specimen was excavated by Mr. Earl Morris in the ruins of a small pueblo built shortly after 1750.

Drawing by Miss Betsy Forbes   Photograph by the Denver Art Museum

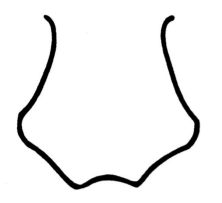

Plate XVI
Ogapoge Polychrome Olla
Height 11½ inches
University of Colorado, 381

PLATE XVII

Ogapoge Polychrome Olla

Form: This jar, apart from a considerably lessened curve to the upward slope of its neck, requires no further attention.

Decoration: Black and red matte paints on a creamy white ground.

The omission of the more usual peripherally placed band of design obviously denotes a breaking away from tradition, as also does the character of decoration. The four units projecting from the corners of each hour-glass shaped figure probably represent turkey feathers.

No ceremonial break is apparent.

Coming from the same ruin as the olla on the preceding plate, it will date circa 1750 or about a half century after Tewa Polychrome was in fashion.

Drawing by Miss Betsy Forbes   Photograph by the Denver Art Museum

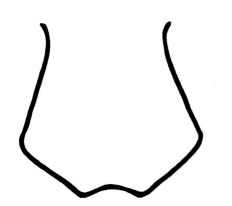

PLATE XVIII

Ogapoge Polychrome Olla

Form: Though some individual variations of form occur within the type none of these appear to have a particular significance and the olla here figured, while proportionately broader than some, comes well within the limit.

Decoration: Black and red matte paints on a creamy white ground.

This example preserves the system of dual decorative areas; a median and that on the neck. As is quite often the case at this time, the designs of the upper area show less conservatism than do those on the lower, the latter harking back to an older order. Here again two forms of feather symbols are included in the decorative scheme on the neck. (See plates XVI and XIX for other examples.) Although a comparatively nice degree of balance and symmetry of design has been attained, minor differences in detail may be seen.

A ceremonial break extends completely through both upper and lower bands of decoration.

This specimen, in its present well used condition, was obtained at the pueblo of Cochiti in the 1880's by A. F. Bandelier, one of the earliest investigators in problems of the Southwest.

Photograph by the Peabody Museum at Harvard University

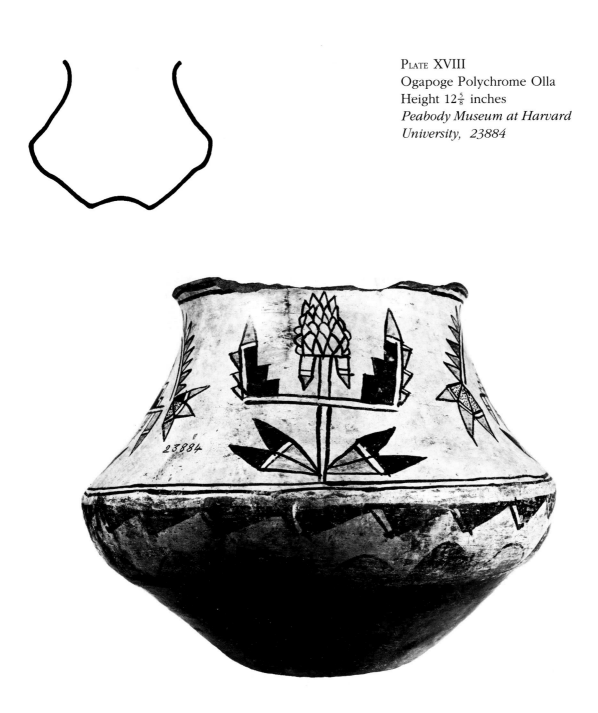

PLATE XVIII
Ogapoge Polychrome Olla
Height 12⅝ inches
*Peabody Museum at Harvard
University, 23884*

PLATE XIX

Ogapoge Polychrome Olla

Form: A form having a shape even more broad in proportion to the height than the example illustrated on the previous plate is here shown.

Decoration: Black and red matte paints on a creamy white ground.

Unfortunately the peripheral zone of decoration in this case is so badly defaced from wear that it has been found impossible to gain any idea concerning the character of the pattern used. The design on the neck shows considerable formality, the various units presenting no differences in detail. Here numerous feather symbols have been made a part of the decorative scheme.

Chipping and erosion of the rim have so destroyed the uppermost framing lines in places that the possibility of a ceremonial break cannot be determined, though there is no opening in the line separating the upper and lower decorative bands.

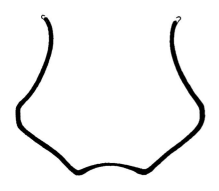

PLATE XIX
Ogapoge Polychrome Olla
Height 11¾ inches
Dr. F. E. Mera collection

PLATE XX

Ogapoge Polychrome Bowl

Form: The rim of this bowl, though having a marked inward slant, preserves the earlier Tewa Polychrome tradition (plate XIV) by still being kept a separate feature, distinct from the balance of the vessel.

Decoration: Black matte paint on a creamy white ground.

The simple tripartite design units have not been identified as conventionalizations of any particular object. On bowls as well as ollas of this period, a zone of red was applied immediately beneath the band of decoration, leaving the rest of the basal portion unslipped.

No ceremonial opening was left in either upper or lower framing lines.

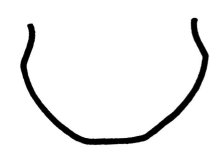

Plate **XX**
Ogapoge Polychrome Bowl
Diameter 14½ inches
Indian Arts Fund, 770

PLATE XXI

Pojoaque Polychrome Olla

Form: Like Ogapoge Polychrome, this type was a development out of the Sankawi-Tewa succession, with a flared rim taken from Posuge Red, and hence agrees in general shape with all the other members in this generic group, which also included Kapo Black (plates XXIV and XXV).

Decoration: Black matte paint on a creamy white ground, highly burnished red neck.

In this type also, the median band of decoration is a prominent feature, the nature of the designs employed being usually stiffly formal and elemental in character. The horizontally placed tapered units in the several panels may within reason be considered as adaptations of feather symbols. See like units on plate LXVI.

A ceremonial break may be seen in the upper framing line.

This specimen came from a site which has been dated 1750+.

Drawing by Miss Betsy Forbes   Photograph by the Denver Art Museum

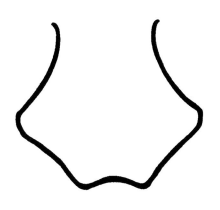

PLATE **XXI**
Pojoaque Polychrome Olla
Height 11½ inches
University of Colorado, 380

PLATE XXII

Pojoaque Polychrome Olla

Form: This example presents no marked deviation from the general run of shapes within the group.

Decoration: Black matte paint on a creamy white ground, highly burnished red neck.

A very simple arrangement of stepped figures comprises the entire decorative scheme for the paneled peripheral band which has been completely divided by a ceremonial break. The two panels immediately to the right of this opening show a non-conformity with all the others in the number of stepped elements.

All Pojoaque Polychrome jars thus far examined have the zone of red below the median band on their underbodies.

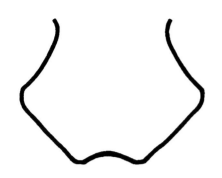

PLATE XXII
Pojoaque Polychrome Olla
Height 11 inches
Indian Arts Fund, 384

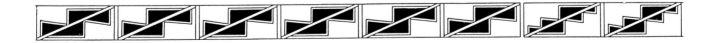

PLATE XXIII

Pojoaque Polychrome Olla

Form: As may be seen, no remarks are required under this head.
Decoration: Black matte paint on a creamy white ground, highly burnished red neck.

A somewhat greater degree of elaboration distinguishes the painted decoration on this jar from the two just previously illustrated. The last three design units to the right have five serrations attached to each arc as against four for all others.

A ceremonial break interrupts the band.

This and the one on the preceding plate were found among a quantity of rubbish in a long disused storage room in the pueblo of Jemez.

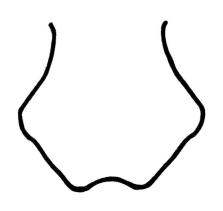

PLATE **XXIII**
Pojoaque Polychrome Olla
Height $11\frac{1}{2}$ inches
Indian Arts Fund, 385

PLATE XXIV

Kapo Black Olla

Form: A considerable degree of flare to the rim is noticeable in this olla although all other features conform to those of its companion types, Ogapoge and Pojoaque Polychromes.

Decoration: Polished black, the result of a deposition of carbon by a process of smudging. This well finished black surface entirely covers the upperbody and also extends down onto the more grayish base to about the same distance as that occupied by the usual red ring in the polychrome types of this same period, probably indicating the application of a red pigment, before firing, to those parts later exhibiting the densest black.

This jar was unearthed in the pueblo of San Ildefonso during the course of some incidental excavation.

PLATE XXV

Kapo Black Olla

Form: The same exaggerated flaring of the rim is as manifest in this example as in the one figured on the preceding plate.

Decoration: Polished black.

Discovered unbroken by A. V. Kidder during his excavation of Pecos Pueblo, in a part of the ruin occupied during the historic period.

PLATE XXVI

Kapo Black Bowl

Form: Bowls of this type retain, in principle, rims following those of the ancestral Tewa Polychrome type (plate XIV), this feature still being held as distinct from the bowl proper.

Decoration: Polished black.

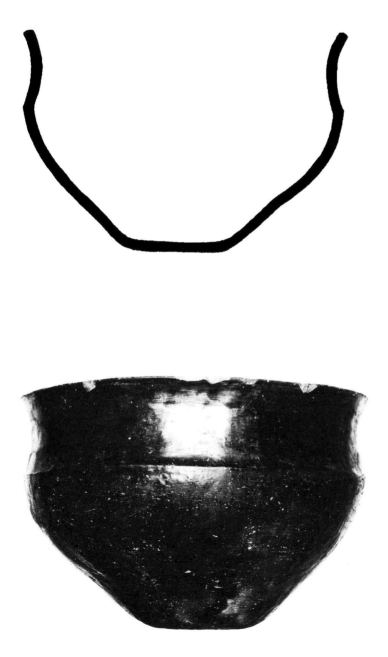

PLATE XXVII

Ogapoge Polychrome Olla, Aberrant Form

Form: A few jars having this shape began to appear in both Upper and Middle Rio Grande provinces as early as the first part of the 18th Century, while the more usual forms were still produced. See plate XXXIV for an example early enough to have received a decoration in glaze paint. Curiously, this form, though seemingly never becoming plentiful enough to be considered in the light of an established type, survived to some extent well into the first part of the 20th Century, particularly in the pueblo of San Ildefonso.

Decoration: Black matte paint on a (due to discoloration) grayish tan base.

What is plainly a variation of the two band system of decoration has been employed on this jar, only the framing lines which would normally separate the upper and lower zones have been omitted. The artist may have felt justified in such a course because the two have evidently been designed to more or less complement one another, an unusual occurrence in typical two band decoration. A design of this character may be viewed as a step towards the all-over patterns of a later day. Another departure from established custom consists of extending the light colored slip, usually confined to the upperbody, down onto the underbody nearly to the vessel's base.

A ceremonial break has been made only in the two lower framing lines.

The reasons for including this specimen are two in number: first, it was found in a rocky niche in a section of country known to have been inhabited by Pueblo refugees in mid-18th Century times; second, the character of design does not conform to any of the well known village specializations which appear to have originated in the early part of the 19th Century. Hence it is tentatively assigned to a time between the middle and end of the 18th.

84

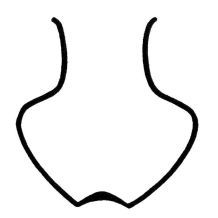

Plate XXVII
Ogapoge Polychrome Olla,
Aberrant Form
Height 10½ inches
Indian Arts Fund, 1160

PLATE XXVIII

Ogapoge Black-on-cream Olla, Aberrant Form

Form: The remarks made concerning the olla shape immediately preceding are equally applicable here. Compare both of these with the cross sections of the Kapo Black jars on plates XXIV and XXV, of which forms these may represent an extreme exaggeration.

Decoration: Black matte paint on a creamy white ground.

As all visible portions of the vessel had been slipped with the usual ground color, it was possible to fully decorate both upper and underbodies. In this connection it may be of interest to know that full slipping, especially of vessels having this shape, was not an uncommon practice in San Ildefonso during the early part of the 20th Century. Two parallel lines extending about the vessel, close to the carinated periphery, divide the field into two bands. In neither one of these is there any appearance of organized design. All that can be made out are several stepped figures in outline. The character of decoration allies it with no particular style, a peculiarity which may be explained when its history is told.

No ceremonial break occurs.

The family from whom it was obtained has lived in the neighborhood of Pecos Pueblo for a number of generations. The owners asserted that it originally came into their possession by gift from a Pecos Indian sometime previous to the abandonment of that village in 1838. If such an origin be accepted, it illustrates to what depths the ceramic art of Pecos had sunk by the first part of the 19th Century.

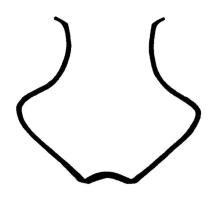

PLATE XXVIII
Ogapoge Black-on-cream Olla,
Aberrant Form
Height $9\frac{1}{4}$ inches
Laboratory of Anthropology, 10/1916

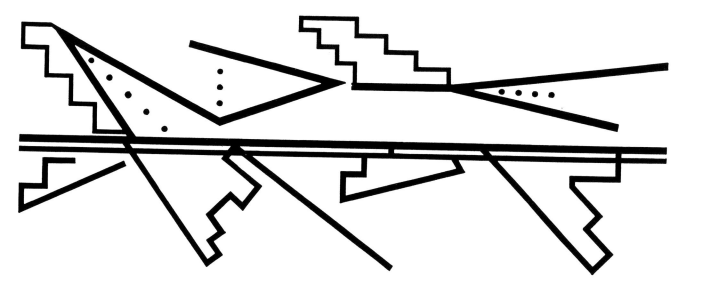

PLATE XXIX

Upper Rio Grande Olla, Aberrant Form

Form: Although here classed as aberrant, this example can only be viewed in that light in so far as the Upper Rio Grande is concerned because it is in other respects a typical form for the glaze-paint area to the south, the type of paint and design alone revealing it to be probably a northern product. Compare this shape with those on plates XXX and XXXI.

Decoration: Black and red matte paints on a creamy white ground.

This is one of the earliest dated examples approaching an all-over treatment which eventually became very popular, though at a much later date, on vessels of this shape in the Upper Rio Grande province. A suggestion of the dual band system, however, can still be seen to persist in the independent narrow band about the neck. Two varieties of feather symbols are incorporated in the medallion, and also attached to the top and bottom framing lines which bound the principal field of decoration.

No ceremonial break appears.

This jar was also secured at the same ruin, dating circa 1750, from which a number of other examples are cited.

Drawing by Miss Betsy Forbes   Photograph by the Denver Art Museum

88

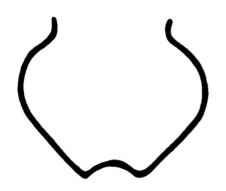

PLATE XXIX
Upper Rio Grande Olla,
Aberrant Form
Height 9¼ inches
University of Colorado, 410

PLATE XXX

Kotyiti Glaze-polychrome Olla

Form: The shape here shown, from a study of sherd material and other data, represents one that comes the nearest to a standardized form developed in the Middle Rio Grande province, after taller shapes and concave bottoms became the fashion. It is obvious that the gain in height was accomplished not by a lengthening of the neck as in the Upper Rio Grande, but by a rounding and an upward extension of the body section. Note the differences between this and the two late prehistoric specimens shown on plates IV and V.

Decoration: Medium to dark brown glaze and red matte paints on a buffy ground.

Not only was there a considerable lack of uniformity in olla shapes during the final appearance of glaze-paint decoration, but an unsettled and chaotic situation as regards design is very apparent. Such a condition seems to be due largely to an attempt to emulate the more elaborate patterns of the Little Colorado area with only an inherited, stiffly formalized system of design upon which to draw. During late prehistoric times in this province, the two band system of decoration (plates IV and V) was a firmly established practice but toward the close of the 17th Century this formula received much less emphasis. In the present instance, the usual band of design about the neck has been reduced to an outlined stripe of red while the lower band partakes more of the nature of an all-over treatment.

There seems to have been no ceremonial break.

This olla was obtained by N. C. Nelson during his excavation of Kotyiti, a village erected by the Cochiti Indians following the Pueblo Rebellion of 1680, which was afterward stormed and destroyed in 1694.

Drawing by the author from a sketch furnished by the American Museum of Natural History

Photograph by the American Museum of Natural History

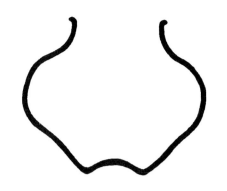

PLATE XXX
Kotyiti Glaze-polychrome Olla
Height 10¼ inches
*American Museum of Natural
History, 29.0/3140*

PLATE XXXI

KOTYITI GLAZE-POLYCHROME OLLA

Form: The shape of this fragmentary olla, as far as can be judged, probably differed to no great extent from the one shown on the preceding plate. The postulated outline of the missing portion, indicated by a thin line, has been added from evidence furnished by a study of sherds from sites of this period. Note the flaring of the rim, an established procedure in this province before it became standard for the Upper Rio Grande.

Decoration: Medium to dark brown glaze and matte red paints on a buff to pinkish ground.

Here again, a greatly altered rendition of the two band system has been used. On the neck, a series of units has been placed at intervals along the lower edge of a single red stripe but with no lower framing line to convert the composition into a true framed decorative band. The body design has a similar construction. Suspended from the former are "key" figures, a device much used in the Middle Rio Grande, alternating with chevron-like arrangements. Besides these "key" units there is little to link the composition as a whole with any to be seen on prehistoric vessels native to this province. For variations of the "key" see plates XXXIV, XXXVI and XXXVII.

A ceremonial break is apparently absent.

This specimen, like the example previously discussed, was secured from the ruined pueblo of Kotyiti (1680–1694).

Drawing by the author from a sketch furnished by the American Museum of Natural History

Photograph by the American Museum of Natural History

92

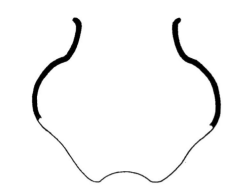

PLATE XXXI
Kotyiti Glaze-polychrome Olla
Diameter 11¾ inches
American Museum of Natural History, 29.0/3099

PLATE XXXII

Kotyiti Glaze-polychrome Olla

Form: A strong influence derived from Upper Rio Grande styles is evident in this specimen. Although the inward sloping neck is shorter and the basal third of the jar is proportionately deeper, the general cross section is not so far removed from some of the shapes belonging in that region. Also, there is more of a beveled treatment of the rim like that of Tewa Polychrome, than there is of the typically flared rims of the middle Rio Grande.

Decoration: Brown glaze and matte red paints on a pinkish tan ground.

Another instance of atypical, dual band decoration. In the present case, the upper or neck band has been made the principal interest while the lower, although there is no bottom framing line, resembles in the manner of treatment those highly stylized lower bands of Ogapoge Polychrome (plates XVI and XVIII), and in which type any exuberance of design, following a further likeness to the present example, was reserved for the upper zone of decoration. The series of diagonal lines below the principal band of design which join to form a zigzag do not complete a balanced pattern, due apparently to a miscalculation in spacing. Feather symbols can be seen incorporated in the several designs of the upper band.

Two ceremonial openings have been made in the framing lines. These were not placed directly opposite one another.

This olla came from a village occupied only during the period of the Pueblo Rebellion, 1680–1694.

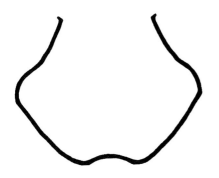

PLATE XXXII
Kotyiti Glaze-polychrome Olla
Height 11 inches
Laboratory of Anthropology, 30/1290

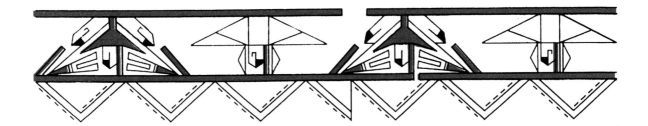

PLATE XXXIII

KOTYITI GLAZE-POLYCHROME OLLA

Form: It is not surprising that many of the jars bearing late styles in glaze-paint decoration, also have shapes more or less closely related to the forms of the nearby Upper Rio Grande as the idea of tall shapes undoubtedly originated in that province. The one here illustrated is a case in point. Compare the cross section of this one with those on plates XVIII and XIX and it will be seen that, except for a slightly greater constriction of the neck, there is a marked similarity.

Decoration: Dark brown glaze and matte red paints on a buffy white ground.

The general plan of decoration is definitely based on the two band system. Design units employed in the median zone are plainly patterned after one of the numerous bird-tail motifs (plate LXVII) frequently used in the two westernmost ceramic provinces. No definite relationship to any particular decorative style can be argued for the band on the neck although four feather symbols, also an adopted unit from the west, are present.

A ceremonial break appears in the framing lines and uppermost portions of both decorative fields.

This specimen dates from about the middle of the 18th Century.

Drawing by Miss Betsy Forbes   Photograph by the Denver Art Museum

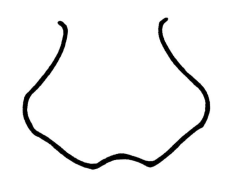

PLATE XXXIII
Kotyiti Glaze-polychrome Olla
Height $9\frac{7}{8}$ inches
University of Colorado, 379

PLATE XXXIV

Kotyiti Glaze-polychrome Olla, Aberrant Form

Form: That this shape was copied from or served as an inspiration for certain unclassed northern forms (plates XXVII and XXVIII) can hardly be questioned, though the extremely flared rim occurring as early as it does in this case, about a half century before the dates tentatively assigned to the two cited northern examples, presupposes the latter.

Decoration: Light brownish glaze and matte red paints on a light tan ground.

Only a vestige of the classic dual band system is to be found, although an analysis of the decorative detail indicates merely a rearrangement of typical Lower Rio Grande design forms to fit a different shaped space. The "key" figure appears prominently.

A ceremonial opening is continuous through the principal design structure but the broad red stripe just below the rim does not extend through.

It was excavated in the ruins of a temporarily inhabited village occupied by San Felipe Indians during and for a short time after the period of the Pueblo Rebellion of 1680. De Vargas visited this pueblo, which was then located high on the mesa above the present town of San Felipe, in 1694, thus providing a clue regarding the age of the specimen here illustrated. It will be of interest to know that while this type of pottery was in use here, the people of San Ildefonso at the same time, as shown by material from Black Mesa (1694) in Upper Rio Grande territory, were concerned principally with the manufacture of Tewa Polychrome (plates XIV and XV).

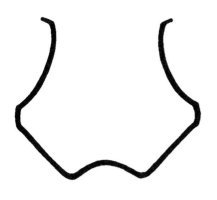

PLATE XXXIV
Kotyiti Glaze-polychrome Olla,
Aberrant Form
Height 8½ inches
Laboratory of Anthropology, 30/1145

PLATE XXXV

KOTYITI GLAZE-POLYCHROME OLLA, Aberrant Form

Form: This example is merely a duplication of the dominant form in the northern Rio Grande district during the late 17th Century and hence may be considered as aberrant for the Middle Rio Grande. Also the flaring of the rim antedates, when its age (late 17th Century) is taken into consideration, any extended use of this style in northern territory where, except for Posuge Red (p. 12), rims were more direct. *Decoration:* Blackish to grayish glaze paint on a semi-polished red ground.

The red polished slip allies this jar with the Posuge Red type, at present only known from sherds, but on none of which has decoration previously been detected by the writer. Another detail pointing toward hybridism is seen in the use of disconnected units just below the rim, separate figures in a like position being often observed as early as Sankawi Black-on-cream. In fact, the whole character and treatment of design hints strongly of a northern influence. Only one section of the median band has been divided into panels, the balance being filled by a running zigzag. Notice the lack of uniformity in the third panel from the left.

No evidence has been obtained concerning a ceremonial break.

This specimen and those shown on plates XXX and XXXI were all secured by N. C. Nelson during the excavation of the village of Kotyiti (1680–1694).

Drawing by the author from data furnished by the American Museum of Natural History

Photograph by the American Museum of Natural History

100

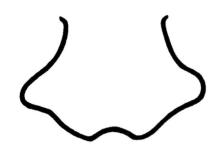

Plate XXXV
Kotyiti Glaze-polychrome Olla,
Aberrant Form
Height 9⅛ inches
*American Museum of Natural
History, 29.0/3144*

PLATE XXXVI

Kotyiti Glaze-polychrome Bowl

Form: A typical bowl shape of the late 17th Century. Compare this and the one on the following plate with a late prehistoric example on plate VI.

Decoration: Dark brown glaze and red matte paints on a deep reddish tan ground.

The entire decorative scheme is typically Middle Rio Grande in character. The units showing a variation of the "key" pattern occupy the exterior of the rim and two of the highly conventionalized bird symbols are to be seen incorporated in the interior design.

Cuaraí, the village from which it was obtained, was abandoned about the year 1674 in consequence of a series of Apache raids.

There is no ceremonial break.

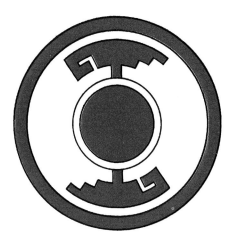

PLATE XXXVI
Kotyiti Glaze-polychrome Bowl
Diameter 13 inches
Indian Arts Fund, 2027

PLATE XXXVII

Kotyiti Glaze-polychrome Bowl

Form: There is little to distinguish the form of this bowl from that illustrated on the preceding plate except for a slightly greater thickening of the rim.

Decoration: Black glaze and red matte paints on a deep reddish tan ground.

In this specimen also, there are neither signs of unusual elaboration in design nor any visible effects of modifications due to outside influences, which are so noticeable on the ollas of this period. Four Middle Rio Grande "key" units are prominent features of the interior decorative scheme.

A ceremonial opening can be seen dividing the pattern on the exterior.

This bowl, together with the three others pictured on plates XIV, XV and XXXII, were all secured at the same site, Astialakwa, which was occupied during the Pueblo Rebellion (1680–1694), showing that the types represented in the group were contemporaneous.

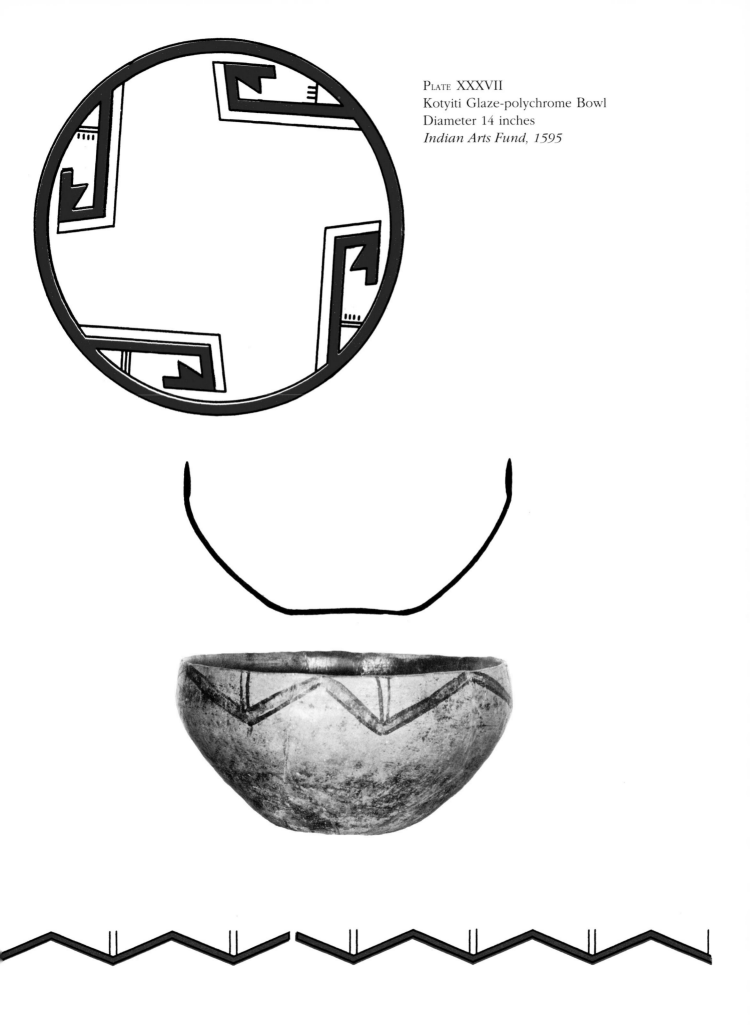

PLATE XXXVII
Kotyiti Glaze-polychrome Bowl
Diameter 14 inches
Indian Arts Fund, 1595

PLATE XXXVIII

Puname Polychrome Olla

Form: Although at first sight this jar may appear to be but a modification of an Upper Rio Grande form, which in part it may be, the angle at which the extremely short neck meets the body tends to confirm a relationship with certain Little Colorado forms (plates LVI and LVIII). This is especially so when a series of this type is examined (plates XXXIX to XLV).

Decoration: Black and red matte paints on a creamy white ground.

Three structurally unrelated bands, the two upper composed of panels, occupy the upperbody. The space separating the superior bands from one another is not greater than that dividing the bands into panels which in reality converts the whole into practically an all-over design. A similar arrangement on a vessel from the Little Colorado province may be seen on plate LVI. Also derived from that western source, are a number of feather symbols which spring from an oblique line in the panels of the lower band.

Below the main design an almost continuous row of arched members may be seen, possibly a refinement based on the zigzag (plates XXXII and XXXIV). These arcs were a popular decorative device in the western part of Middle Rio Grande territory (plates XLI, XLII and XLV).

A ceremonial opening breaks both the upper and lowermost framing lines of the principal design and also interrupts the series of arcs below it, where some extra curved lines have been added.

A date of 1750 + has been secured for the ruin from which this specimen came.

Drawing by Miss Betsy Forbes   Photograph by the Denver Art Museum

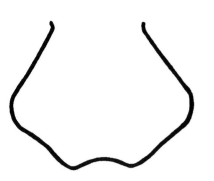

Plate XXXVIII
Puname Polychrome Olla
Height $10\frac{7}{8}$ inches
University of Colorado, 382

PLATE XXXIX

Puname Polychrome Olla

Form: The cross section of this olla does not differ materially from that shown on the previous plate, requiring in consequence, no further remarks.

Decoration: Black and red matte paints on a creamy white ground.

An all-over treatment or perhaps a single band, as distinguished from the multiple zone idea, is plainly apparent. Note the small differences of structural detail occurring in two of the pendant units of design attached to the red stripe circling the vessel just below the neck, in which a break has been made.

Although no exact date is available, this jar has been included, as it was found in association with the one illustrated on plate XXVII. The two had been hidden beneath a rocky overhang in a district known to have been inhabited by bands of Pueblo refugees about the middle of the 18th Century, from which, in addition to a few whole pieces, many sherds representative of the styles of that period have been secured.

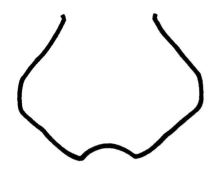

PLATE XL

PUNAME POLYCHROME OLLA

Form: A typically abbreviated neck is well shown here. Less usual is the approach to an angle at which the upperbody meets the basal portion.

Decoration: Black and red matte paints on a creamy white ground.

Sometime between the middle of the 18th and perhaps the first part of the 19th Century, a certain formula for laying out designs originated in the two western towns of the Middle Rio Grande province, Tsia and Santa Ana. As a basic procedure, the field to be decorated was divided into four horizontal panels, two long alternating with two much shorter. (See also plates XLII to XLV.) In this particular instance the two minor panels are drawn obliquely to the vertical axis of the jar. In detail, a strictly balanced arrangement of color was not carried out in the two smaller panels. Such arbitrary divisions do not seem to have survived for any great length of time into the 19th Century when less formal designs executed with greater freedom came into use.

A ceremonial break may be seen extending entirely through the zone of decoration.

This olla came from a long unused storage room in the pueblo of Jemez and as far as can be judged on the evidence of sherds should date perhaps as late as circa 1800.

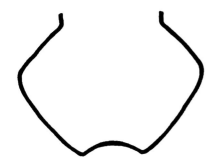

PLATE XLI

Puname Polychrome Olla

Form: In the jar here shown, that part usually taking the form of a short neck is flared to such an extent that it has been practically transformed into more of a rim but as the general shape and character of design conform to the Puname type it has been thought best to include it as a variant.

Decoration: Black and red matte paints on a pinkish tan ground.

Whether this design can be viewed as an attenuation of the old two band system is uncertain but if it can be so regarded, any such relationship would probably be remote. Of the five panels into which the principal decorative band is divided, no two are exactly alike. In some of these, feather symbols occupy a prominent position.

Below the row of double arc units, here having their ends more widely separated than is usually the case, a perfunctorily applied red ring encircles the jar which, as before explained while discussing some of the upper Rio Grande types, came to replace a coat of that color applied to the entire basal section of ollas, a practice finally adopted in both eastern ceramic provinces.

A break extends almost through the whole width of the upper band of decoration, only the lower framing line being left intact.

This was accidentally unearthed in the pueblo of Jemez.

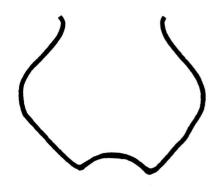

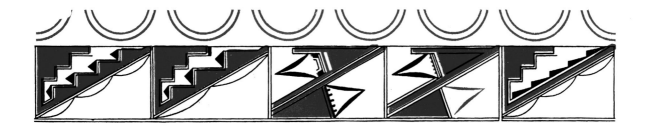

PLATE XLII

PUNAME POLYCHROME OLLA

Form: This is a shape which combines the more globular contours, a preference of the Middle Rio Grande province, with the short upright neck derived from a Little Colorado source.

Decoration: Black and red matte paints on a creamy white slip.

Here again four panels, alternately long and short, compose the principal band of decoration, in which a number of elaborately conceived feather symbols will be noted. These resemble, in the use of red within the outline of each feather, others occurring in designs on Little Colorado vessels shown on plates LVIII and LX. Another device common to both regions is an open space in which a dot was centered. Such openings were apparently used to break the monotony of solidly filled areas. These are often round, though there is also a rectangular version. Openings having a crescentic outline, as here exemplified, are more rare. For other examples consult plates XLIII, XLIV, XLV, LV, LVII and LXI.

Although there is a good degree of balance and symmetry of design, a number of differences as regards detail exist and the inverted arched units below are not placed in any fixed relation to the panel division above them.

The ceremonial break completely divides the decorative band just to the right of the first short panel.

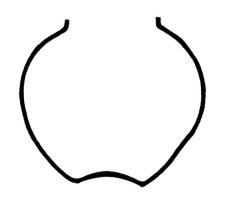

PLATE XLII
Puname Polychrome Olla
Height 10½ inches
Indian Arts Fund, 1569

PLATE XLIII

Puname Polychrome Olla

Form: One of the more globular forms. The short neck possesses a barely perceptible exterior flanging of the lip.

Decoration: Black and matte red paints on a creamy white ground.

The basic long and short panel arrangement is again evident in this specimen. Note the two feather derivatives in the lower halves of both short panels.

To the right of the short panel on the left a complete break may be seen.

It is peculiar that a majority of all the unbroken specimens of the Puname type have been found in localities other than those in which it was manufactured, but a study of material from the trash deposits of Tsia and Santa Ana proves beyond question that such were the places of origin.

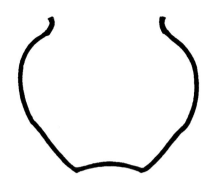

PLATE XLIII
Puname Polychrome Olla
Height 9 inches
Indian Arts Fund, 84

PLATE XLIV

PUNAME POLYCHROME OLLA

Form: Although a more elongate form, the general shape and rudimentary neck would place this specimen in the Puname group.

Decoration: Black and red matte paints on a creamy white ground.

A large measure of simplicity characterizes the structure of this long-and-short panel design. The two horizontally placed pointed design units in each short panel can be traced, through a series of changes, as an abstraction of certain feather symbols. Also note how the row of arcs have undergone a transformation from the more simple form heretofore shown and have been shifted from a position below the principal decorative band to one above it.

Only the bottom framing line has not been parted by the ceremonial break, which otherwise passes through both the band of design and line of arc units.

This jar is believed, from a study of sherd material, to date somewhere in the first part of the 19th Century, and in the character of design resembles styles more particularly associated with the pueblo of Santa Ana. All other examples of the Puname type illustrated appear to have originated in Tsia.

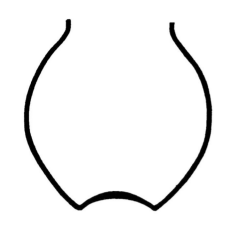

Plate XLIV
Puname Polychrome Olla
Height 12 inches
Indian Arts Fund, 27

PLATE XLV

Puname Polychrome Olla

Form: Another of the taller shapes is here shown. The short neck is flared outward making it difficult to determine whether that feature should not, in this case, be classed as merely a rim. Nevertheless, a summing up of all characteristics makes this jar assignable to no other group and it is therefore retained here.

Decoration: Black and red matte paints on a creamy white ground.

The general scheme of design corresponds with the one figured on plate XLII. In the present instance there is perhaps a greater intricacy of detail but the most interesting departure from a normal procedure may be seen in the areas splotched with red, obviously an attempt to reproduce the stippled effects common to Hopi yellow wares. (See plate LXVII.)

The entire field of decoration is traversed vertically by a ceremonial gap.

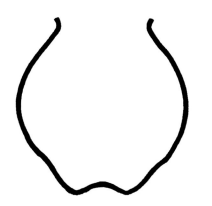

PLATE XLV
Puname Polychrome Olla
Height 13 inches
Fred Harvey collection

PLATE XLVI

Puname Polychrome Bowl

Form: Strictly speaking, the above term was primarily intended to designate a some-what heterogeneous group of olla shapes, eight examples of which have been just previously pictured. There is perhaps no reason why the same designation, with certain restrictions, cannot be used to include bowls produced during the life of that fashion. As bowl shapes based on the principle of a rim separate from the balance of the vessel survived on into the 20th Century, a line of separation must be made to distinguish the early from the later forms, heretofore commonly included under the term Tsia Polychrome. Without wishing to trespass beyond the time horizon set as the upper limit for this paper, it will be best to briefly call attention to a promi-nent feature that will help to distinguish the later forms from the example shown here. Broadly, the difference lies in the style of rim, which in the later fashion is always much higher in proportion to the depth of the bowl and tends to flare more widely than do the comparatively short and more vertical sort of an earlier day. For ancestral Middle Rio Grande forms from which both the present and those later shapes with the expanded rims were derived, see plates XXXVI and XXXVII.

Decoration: Black and red matte paints on a creamy white ground.

On the exterior of the rim are five design units in red which are variations of the familiar Middle Rio Grande "key" figure. The decoration within the bowl is based on the alternating long-and-short panel idea. Practically the entire decora-tive structure used in ornamenting the long panels is based on a combination of feather symbols.

There is no ceremonial break in the design.

A date circa 1750 has been obtained for this bowl.

Drawing by Miss Betsy Forbes   Photograph by the Denver Art Museum

122

Plate XLVI
Puname Polychrome Bowl
Diameter 15¼ inches
University of Colorado, 384

PLATE XLVII

Hawikuh Polychrome Olla

Form: This olla form is typical of the style in use in the Little Colorado ceramic province from the latest part of the prehistoric period until after the opening of the 18th Century. Note the specialization of rim and lip. There is plainly little relationship between the shapes of this district and those of the Middle Rio Grande (plates IV and V), except for rounded bottoms.

Decoration: Black glaze and red matte paints on both a red (body) and creamy white (neck) ground.

Usually two separate and unrelated bands of design were employed, one just beneath the rim, the other encircling the jar at its greatest circumference, although other arrangements are also known. When the band system was used, these were normally broken up into panels, especially so for the lower zone. Feather symbols of various sorts, as may be seen here, were very frequently used as details in design structures.

The ceremonial break is confined to the two topmost lines framing the median band of decoration and does not affect the neck band at all.

This example was discovered in the pueblo of Acoma.

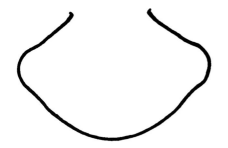

PLATE XLVIII

Hawikuh Glaze-on-red Olla

Form: Another example of this type in which there is a very pronounced thickening of the rim.

Decoration: Black glaze paint on a red ground.

As there are but two colors on this olla the term polychrome is out of place, hence the above name is substituted, although no generic difference is inferred as apart from others in this group. Slipping of the entire vessel in the desired color was the accepted practice. The dual band decorative scheme is here again exemplified, as also is the use of feather symbols, which may be seen in the lower band. This particular form is presumed to be a conventionalization of an eagle's tail feather by reason of a similarity in markings.* Note the change from serrations to elongate dots in the rectangle to the left of the solid semilunar unit farthest to the right and also that such a feature in any form has been omitted in connection with the next similarly curved unit to the left.

Two ceremonial breaks occur, one involving the lower part of the upper band, the other, only the two upper lines of the lower. These openings do not lie opposite one another.

A search of the pueblo of Acoma yielded this jar.

* Chapman, 1927, pp. 526–540.

126

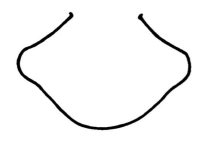

Plate XLVIII
Hawikuh Glaze-on-red Olla
Height 11 inches
Indian Arts Fund, 996

PLATE XLIX

Hawikuh Polychrome Olla

Form: As this olla conforms to the usual pattern no remarks are necessary.

Decoration: Greenish glaze and matte red paints on a creamy white ground.

Although the two band idea is retained, considerable modification has taken place. A very narrow space is all that serves to separate the two and only the upper band is fully framed, the various units of design in the lower being pendant from an upper line, an arrangement which the designer apparently felt required no limiting line at the bottom. Among these units, elaborated feather forms are conspicuous.

A break in the lower framing line of the upper band and the topmost line of the lower forms an opening joining the two, which undoubtedly bears the same significance as the usual gap. Still another may be seen severing the lower of the two topmost framing lines bounding the upper band, a little to the left of the other break.

The pueblo of Acoma yielded this specimen.

Photograph by the Peabody Museum at Harvard University

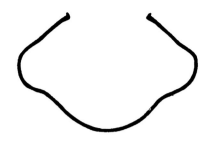

PLATE XLIX
Hawikuh Polychrome Olla
Height 9 inches
*Peabody Museum at Harvard
University, 87410*

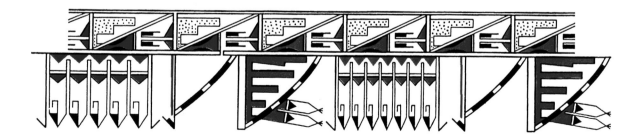

PLATE L

Hawikuh Glaze-on-red Olla

Form: No unusual features need comment.

Decoration: Black glaze paint on a red ground.

The two band idea of decoration is retained although the one about the neck is of such a nature that no lower framing line was needed.

There are several variations in the execution of detail that bespeak a disregard for uniformity. The number of fringe elements on the design units that form the neck band varies from four to five and other discrepancies may be seen in the last two panels at the right end of the principal band. In the first of these the fret pattern has broken down and in the last the serrations are in outline instead of being solid.

A rare occurrence exists in the presence of two distinct ceremonial breaks affecting the lower band, one divides only the two top framing lines, the other, a short distance to the right, not only opens through these same lines but penetrates a third and opens directly into the panel itself.

This specimen was secured at Acoma.

130

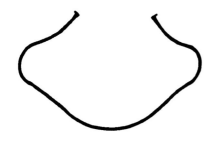

PLATE L
Hawikuh Glaze-on-red Olla
Height 9½ inches
Indian Arts Fund, 1185

PLATE LI

Hawikuh Glaze-on-red Olla

Form: No comments on form are necessary.

Decoration: Green glaze paint on a red ground.

An extreme delicacy of line, when the medium is considered, marks this as an unusual piece. The design, if not a direct copy, shows an exceedingly strong influence from the Hopi ceramic province. A few small deviations from an exact uniformity for the several figures of design do not detract from the general excellence. Feather symbols play an important part in the design structure.

There is no ceremonial break.

A small cavity occurring in an old lava flow in Zuñi territory was the hiding place of this olla.

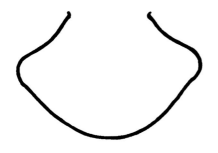

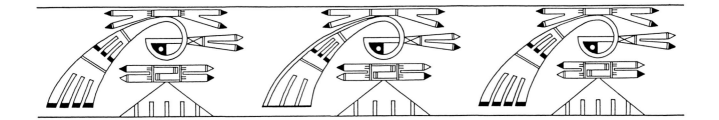

PLATE LII

Hawikuh Polychrome Bowl

Form: Bowls belonging to the Hawikuh type have a rim and lip very similar to those found on jars. In fact, if the usual neck were superimposed on the present example the general shape, excepting the flat bottom, would approximate those within the range of olla forms. The unrounded bottom is indicative of a date toward the final stage of this type, as flat bottoms were common in the following development (plate LXV).

Decoration: Green glaze and matte red paints on a ground originally creamy white.

Below the zone of design, the entire basal portion was slipped with red. A faint trace of the two band system remains, though these have become largely coalescent. Feather motifs are a principal interest in the paneled design structure.

Due to abrasion from wear, parts of the design have disappeared, making it impossible to determine the presence of a ceremonial break. When this bowl was obtained at Acoma, it was still in use, being particularly esteemed for the raising of bread dough, probably because it had become, through long continued use, heavily impregnated with yeast cells.

PLATE LII
Hawikuh Polychrome Bowl
Diameter 12½ inches
Indian Arts Fund, 935

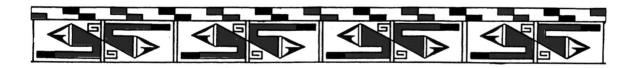

PLATE LIII

Hawikuh Polychrome Bowl

Form: The shape of this bowl varies in no essential way from the one shown on the preceding plate. Hence, the observations made in that instance apply equally well here.

Decoration: Black glaze and red matte paints on a creamy white ground, basal portion red.

In this case decoration is confined to only a single paneled band in which feather symbols occupy a prominent place. Some of these are a part of a stylized bird form.

A ceremonial opening interrupts the top framing line alone.

Like the previous example, this bowl was purchased at Acoma.

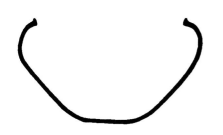

PLATE LIII
Hawikuh Polychrome Bowl
Diameter 12 inches
Olive Rush collection

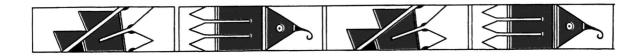

PLATE LIV

Ashiwi Polychrome Olla

Form: In this type a complete reversal of neck form has taken place. Instead of being slightly concave in section, as in the previous Hawikuh type, this feature is now strongly convex. Though at first the rim and lip forms of that earlier style were retained, later, as will be seen, these become less specialized, more direct and finally evolve into a rudimentary neck. In consequence of such a change, that part of the vessel originally a convex neck eventually became the upper part of a more or less globular body. Ollas of this period also show the hollowed out depression in the bottom, an importation from the east, which replaced the previously rounded sort.

Decoration: Black glaze and red matte paints on a burnt orange ground, the entire basal portion slipped with red.

This is the only known example of this type on which glaze paint decoration appears.

Two coalescent bands form the basic structure of design, perhaps a concession to the old pattern, although if so, the entire field of decoration has been displaced upward from the normal of the preceding type to a position above the peripheral bulge.

This specimen illustrates one of two distinctly different ideas concerning the placement of ornamentation during the life of the Ashiwi type. For other examples expressing this same idea see plates LVIII, LX and LXI. In each of these the basal slip has been carried up far enough to include the vessel's bulge. Still another system includes that part within the decorative field.

In the present case, the bands are divided into small panels, eight in the upper and ten in the lower. There has been no attempt to relate the designs in the several panels to a coordinated decorative scheme for the whole, each panel being treated as a separate unit. In some of these, feather symbols have been incorporated.

A ceremonial break in the topmost framing line opens into a space between two vertical lines separating panels in both upper and lower bands, and is continuous to the bottom framing line which has been left intact.

138

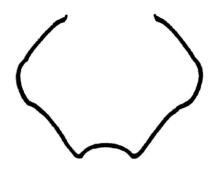

Plate LIV
Ashiwi Polychrome Olla
Height $11\frac{1}{2}$ inches
Indian Arts Fund, 1032

PLATE LV

Ashiwi Polychrome Olla

Form: Although varying somewhat in basal contour from the example illustrated on the previous plate, this olla in other respects comes well within the range of shapes included in the type.

Decoration: Brown and red matte paints on a creamy white ground.

No trace of the dual band system remains here and evidences of paneling are slight, so much so that at first glance, an all-over treatment might be assumed. Nevertheless, the field of decoration has been definitely divided into two parts in the center of which are compositions featuring conventionalized bird forms. A separation of the two areas has been indicated by means of an arrangement of stepped figures dependent from the upper framing line which do not, however, descend far enough to completely form true panels. The designer appears to have still been somewhat influenced by the custom requiring formal divisions.

The ceremonial break affects only the two uppermost framing lines.

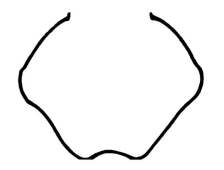

PLATE LV
Ashiwi Polychrome Olla
Height $9\frac{1}{2}$ inches
Indian Arts Fund, 1618

PLATE LVI

Ashiwi Polychrome Olla

Form: Except for a peripherally located bulge the general outline shown in this cross section more nearly approaches the globular than any other of this type known to the writer.

Decoration: Black and red matte paints on a creamy white ground.

The arrangement of the two bands of decoration offers quite a contrast to the former and more usual usage of the Little Colorado province (plates XLVII to L), wherein the upper or neck band was, at best, only equal to or most frequently, of less importance than the lower. The order is here reversed, something after the manner of the styles incident to Ogapoge Polychrome (plates XVI and XVIII), the lower band being represented only by a series of unframed detached figures. In the paneled upper band, at the bottom of the first and third panels from the left, as well as in the detached figures beneath it, may be seen variations of the Middle Rio Grande "key" (plate XXXVI). The remaining panels contain designs in which feather symbols occupy a prominent position. Note differences in the detail of the detached figures.

Immediately to the right of the panel on the extreme left, a ceremonial opening has been made which interrupts all horizontal lines except the topmost.

This piece has a date of circa 1750.

Drawing by Miss Betsy Forbes   Photograph by the Denver Art Museum

142

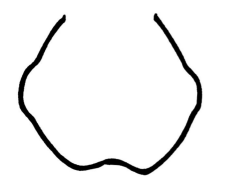

PLATE LVI
Ashiwi Polychrome Olla
Height 10⅜ inches
University of Colorado, 409

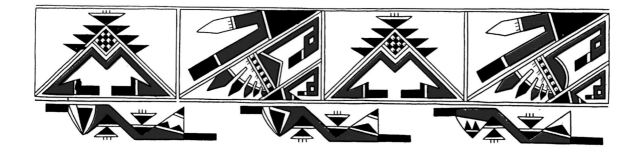

PLATE LVII

Ashiwi Polychrome Olla

Form: No discussion of this typical shape is necessary.

Decoration: Black and red matte paints on a white ground.

Although the structural features of this design are obviously based on the two band idea, in reality there are three of these, if a certain amount of isolation and a disagreement, in two of the uppermost panels, with the general character of design be taken into consideration. The upper part of the superior band is not only separated from the lower portion by a pair of broken framing lines but its panels contain design units based on the ubiquitous "key" motif of the Middle Rio Grande district (plate XXXVI) which inject a note foreign to the rest of the design. Beneath this, all is typically Little Coloradoan, including groups of feather symbols in series, after the manner shown on plate XLIX.

Near the center of the drawing a ceremonial break may be seen extending through all bands to the lowermost framing lines which remain undivided.

A fortunate find in a cave situated in Zuñi territory is responsible for the inclusion of this fine specimen.

144

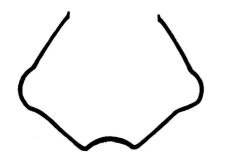

PLATE LVII
Ashiwi Polychrome Olla
Height $9\frac{1}{4}$ inches
Laboratory of Anthropology, 10/1942

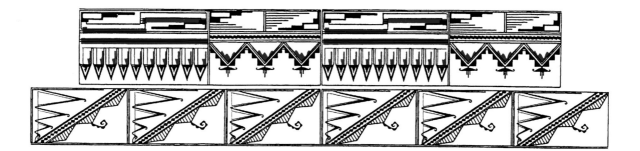

PLATE LVIII

Ashiwi Polychrome Olla

Form: The shape of this jar, a reconstructed cross section of which has been attempted from an average for the type, needs no comment.

Decoration: Black and red matte paints on a creamy white ground.

Here only a single zone of decoration was used, the bulge of the vessel, often ornamented with bands of design, being slipped instead with the same red used to cover the underbody, resulting in a continuous polished surface of that color from the bottom up to the base of the neck. The band is not divided into panels, a running design having been substituted. Feather symbols are again in evidence.

As some sections of this olla are missing, it has been impossible to determine whether there had been a break in the pattern or framing lines.

This is another example dated as having been in use about the middle of the 18th Century.

Drawing by Miss Betsy Forbes   Photograph by the Denver Art Museum

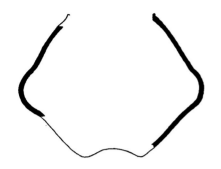

PLATE LVIII
Ashiwi Polychrome Olla
Diameter 12 inches
University of Colorado, 445

PLATE LIX

Ashiwi Polychrome Olla

Form: The only feature deserving especial attention, is the neck which ends in a direct unspecialized rim and lip, a rare occurrence as far as known.

Decoration: Black and red matte paints on a white ground.

The more conservative dual band arrangement divided into panels is evident, although the upper, as noted in explaining plate LVI, has become the center of interest. There is an unusual degree of intricacy and diversity manifest in the pattern as a whole and the artist has accomplished her object so well that in detail no two panels in either band are exactly alike. Both conventionalized birds and feathers have been used with good effect.

No signs of a ceremonial break can be found.

One of the few examples of its period secured at the pueblo of Zuñi.

148

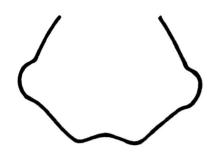

PLATE LIX
Ashiwi Polychrome Olla
Height 9 inches
Indian Arts Fund, 1

PLATE LX

Ashiwi Polychrome Olla

Form: Attention is particularly directed to the rim, which, though still bearing some resemblance to others of this type heretofore shown, has lost all the usual thickening and is slightly upturned to form a narrow flange. This example illustrates a transitional stage that merges with a form in which the rim becomes a neck, as will be seen in the two following plates.

Decoration: Brown and red matte paints on a creamy white ground.

Only a single paneled band has been used in this case in which two compositions, greatly differing in character of design, appear alternately. The second and fourth panels show adaptations of certain Hopi bird abstractions, examples of which may be seen on plate LXVII. Note the disparity between the number of feathers in the two and the height to which the basal slip has been carried.

Due to erosion and flaking, it has been impossible to determine whether an opening once existed in the upper framing lines, though none occurs in the lower.

This specimen was obtained at Acoma.

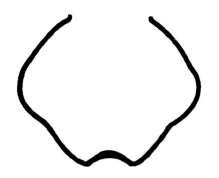

PLATE LX
Ashiwi Polychrome Olla
Height 12 inches
Indian Arts Fund, 999

PLATE LXI

Ashiwi Polychrome Olla

Form: The cross section here shown demonstrates the complete transformation of what was once a rim into a variety of short neck, that portion originally a neck having become a part of the body. It is believed that forms such as this were responsible for much of the character of the Puname Polychrome type (plates XXXVIII to XLV), native to the western part of the Middle Rio Grande province. *Decoration:* Black matte paint on a creamy white ground.

The single band of decoration, although separated into two divisions, can hardly be considered as truly paneled. The arrangement of alternating disassociated design units is similar to that illustrated on the previous plate. Of these the largest and most conspicuous is an elaboration based on a coil, which is remotely derived from a bird abstraction originating in Zuñi, popularly called the Rain Bird.* Observe that the basal slip has been extended well up onto the body of the jar.

A gap in the upper framing lines is the only opening showing the observance of that characteristic convention.

This specimen was acquired at the pueblo of Acoma.

* Mera, 1937.

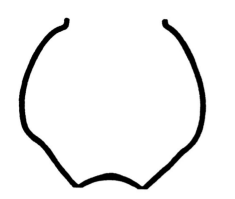

PLATE LXI
Ashiwi Polychrome Olla
Height 12 inches
Laboratory of Anthropology, 10/345

PLATE LXII

Ashiwi Polychrome Olla

Form: The well developed, though comparatively short neck, probably represents the culminating form in this type, before alterations in style brought into fashion the well known shapes characteristic of more recent times. It can be seen by referring to the several preceding plates, on which other examples of the Ashiwi type are figured, that any changes responsible for the alteration of orificial features did not succeed in markedly modifying the shape of body or base.

Decoration: Black, red and orange matte paints on a creamy white ground.

Only a hint of the two band idea remains in the double row of figures that are used in the single zone field of decoration. The units of the lower row may be another modification of the Hopi bird motif that consists of a cross member, often more or less crescentic in form, from which feather symbols depend (plates LV and LXVII). In the present case only a single elaborate feather has been used instead of the usual two or more of less complex structure.

The ceremonial break interrupts the two uppermost black lines but does not affect any part of the design below that point.

154

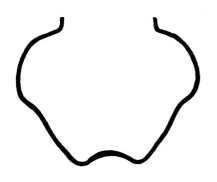

PLATE LXII
Ashiwi Polychrome Olla
Height 10 inches
Indian Arts Fund, 1009

PLATE LXIII

Ashiwi Polychrome Olla, Aberrant Form

Form: The shape of this jar appears to stem, in gross outline, more directly from the glaze-paint Hawikuh type (plates XLVII to LI), except for proportionate height. The character of rim and a basal depression and the slightly concave neck at once separate it from the Ashiwi Polychrome series just figured (plates LIV to LXII). Yet those three exceptions, as well as the paint and character of design, all agree most closely with the latter type, which would seem to argue strongly for a like incidence in time.

Decoration: Black and red matte paints on a white ground.

As in some others in the Ashiwi group, also from the pueblo of Zuñi (plates LVII and LIX), a two band system of decoration was employed, the superior having a greater width than the lower. Unfortunately much of the pattern comprised in the former has disappeared from erosive agencies and little can be made out except that there were many irregularities in minor details. In the lower band, on the contrary, exact duplication and balance has been meticulously carried out. Stylized feathers in pairs are attached to either end of the diamond shaped design units.

A ceremonial opening has been left in the two uppermost framing lines and also another, below and a little farther to the right, forms a passageway connecting the upper and inferior bands.

Collected by James Stevenson in 1879 at the pueblo of Zuñi.

Photograph by the United States National Museum

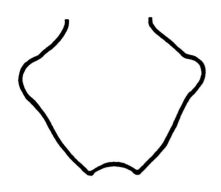

PLATE LXIII
Ashiwi Polychrome Olla,
Aberrant Form
Height 8⅞ inches
*United States National Museum,
41149*

PLATE LXIV

Ashiwi Polychrome Olla, Aberrant Form

Form: Although the shape of this specimen is largely Upper Rio Grande (plates XVI to XVIII), to the tall neck has been added some of the convexity characteristic of Ashiwi Polychrome which has resulted in an interesting case of hybridism. Further evidence regarding its status as a Little Colorado form, however, is apparent in both slip and decoration.

Decoration: Black and red matte paints on a white ground.

This is another example where the two band system has been so treated that virtually three have resulted. See also plate LVII. The topmost band has been badly disfigured and a section of the jar including the rim is missing, making the design difficult to follow in its entirety. It is plain, however, that no attempt was made to duplicate the patterns in its several panels. As a matter of fact, the artist seemed to have exerted considerable effort to avoid repetition in many parts of the field. Note the diversity of decorative devices used to fill in each of a connected row of feather symbols forming the central band and a similar tendency to irregularity in the lowermost zone.

The only ceremonial opening now to be detected can be seen in the two upper lines of the lowest band.

Collected by Matilda Coxe Stevenson in Zuñi.

Photograph by the United States National Museum

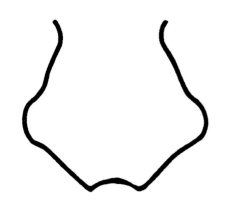

PLATE LXIV
Ashiwi Polychrome Olla,
Aberrant Form
Height 11 inches
*United States National Museum,
234459*

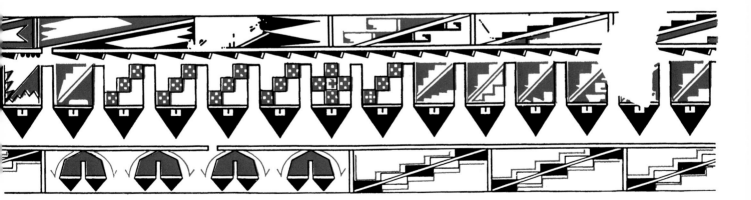

PLATE LXV

Ashiwi Polychrome Bowl

Form: There appears to have been no single standard for bowl shapes as far as a study of available material would indicate. The example here shown has a cross section that suggests the lower half of an olla of the period, except for the absence of a basal depression. Such a form relates more closely to some of those belonging to the Hawikuh glaze-paint type (plates LII and LIII) than do the round bottomed sorts also in use during the life of Ashiwi Polychrome. So few whole specimens or large sherds are known that it is not possible to say anything definite concerning the entire range of shapes nor the relative popularity of one over the others.

Decoration: Black and red matte paints on a white ground.

Decoration of both the interiors and exteriors of bowls was a frequent practice during the period. That on the exterior seems usually to have consisted of a paneled band. In the present case, three of the four divisions are, with a few minor differences in detail, practically duplicates, the remaining panel differing considerably except in general arrangement. Feather symbols may be seen incorporated in the central section of the design on the interior of the bowl.

Paired vertical framing lines separate the several panels, two of which enclose a space open at top and bottom that constitutes a ceremonial break.

This piece was obtained at Zuñi.

160

PLATE LXV
Ashiwi Polychrome Bowl
Diameter 13 inches
Indian Arts Fund, 17

PLATE LXVI

Ashiwi Polychrome Bowl

Form: One of the round bottomed bowls also in use, as explained in the remarks accompanying the preceding plate, during the existence of the Ashiwi type of olla. *Decoration:* Black and red matte paints on a creamy white ground.

As in the previous example, exterior decoration has also been based on the paneled band. Within each space there are design units which, in a general way, resemble certain highly conventionalized bird forms frequently used on Middle Rio Grande glaze-paint vessels (plates V and XXXVI). In the present instance the hook-like heads have been replaced by two feather symbols. A number of other forms of this symbol can also be distinguished among the complexities of the design which go to make up the interior decoration.

No ceremonial opening appears in the drawing.

All criteria point to the Little Colorado province, with the strongest probability of the pueblo of Acoma as the place of origin, although excavated far to the north of that locality. The specimen was unearthed together with the other examples illustrated on plates XVI, XVII, XXI, XXIX, XXXIII, XXXVIII, LVI and LVIII, at a small, temporarily occupied site. This group should give an excellent idea of the various pottery types in use about the middle of the 18th Century.

Drawing by Miss Betsy Forbes   Photograph by the Denver Art Museum

162

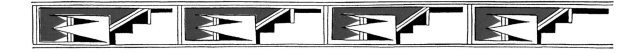

PLATE LXVII

Hopi Feather and Bird Motifs

All the figures shown on the opposite plate have been taken from Jesse Walter Fewkes' "Archaeological Expedition to Arizona in 1895", published as a section of the Seventeenth Annual Report of the Bureau of American Ethnology, Part 2, pages 519–742, Washington, 1898.

The original plate and figure numbers, from which these were copied, are given from left to right, beginning with the top row.

Plate CXXIII, c	Plate CXXXIX, a	Figure 273
Plate CXLI, d	Figure 323	Figure 272
Plate CXLI, e	Plate CXLIV, a	Plate CXLIX, a

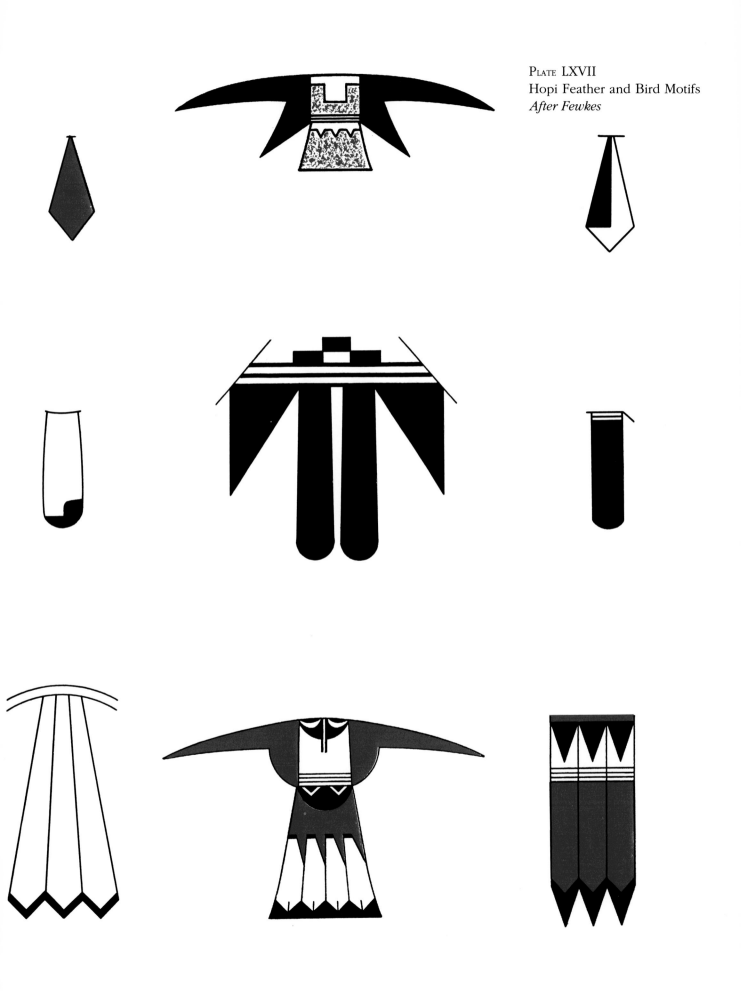

PLATE LXVII
Hopi Feather and Bird Motifs
After Fewkes